Artful Journals

Artful Journals

Making and Embellishing Memory Books, Garden Diaries & Travel Albums

Written and Illustrated
by Janet Takahashi

A LARK/CHAPELLE BOOK

A Division of Sterling Publishing Co., Inc.
New York / London

Editor: Kathy Sheldon
Assistant Editors: Mark Bloom, Julie Hale, Catherine Risling
Design: Susan McBride
Assistant Designer: Shannon Yokeley
Illustrations: Janet Takahashi
Photography: Zachary Williams, John Widman

A Lark/Chapelle Book

Chapelle, Ltd., Inc.
P.O. Box 9255, Ogden, UT 84409
(801) 621-2777 • (801) 621-2788 Fax
e-mail: chapelle@chapelleltd.com
Web site: www.chapelleltd.com

Library of Congress Cataloging-in-Publication Data

Takahashi, Janet, 1952-
  Artful journals : making & embellishing memory books, garden diaries &
travel albums / Janet Takahashi. -- 1st ed.
     p. cm.
  Includes index.
  ISBN 1-60059-069-1 (hardcover)
  1. Photographs--Conservation and restoration. 2. Scrapbook journaling. 3.
Photograph albums. I. Title.
  TR465.T285 2007
  745.593--dc22

                        2006034173

10 9 8 7 6 5 4 3 2 1

First Edition

Published by Lark Books, A Division of Sterling Publishing Co., Inc., 387 Park Avenue South, New York, N.Y. 10016

Text © 2007, Janet Takahashi
Photography © 2007, Lark Books
Illustrations © 2007, Janet Takahashi

Distributed in Canada by Sterling Publishing, c/o Canadian Manda Group, 165 Dufferin Street, Toronto, Ontario, Canada M6K 3H6

Distributed in the United Kingdom by GMC Distribution Services, Castle Place, 166 High Street, Lewes, East Sussex, England BN7 1XU

Distributed in Australia by Capricorn Link (Australia) Pty Ltd., P.O. Box 704, Windsor, NSW 2756 Australia

Manufactured in China

ISBN 13: 978-1-60059-069-6
ISBN 10: 1-60059-069-1

For information about custom editions, special sales, premium and corporate purchases, please contact Sterling Special Sales Department at 800-805-5489 or specialsales@sterlingpub.com.

Table of Contents

The Projects

Introduction

I stood at the edge of the vineyard, eyeing the luscious view before me, trying to settle on one thing to draw quickly. My journal resting on my forearm, travel watercolor box in one hand and a brush in the other, I painted in quick bursts. A group of people gathered to watch and ask questions. Encouraged by the simplicity of the materials I take into the field, they made promises to begin their own journals.

All around my house, in my studio, and tucked into backpacks, I have a multitude of journals in progress—different topics, sizes, and shapes. If you peeked between the covers of my journals, you'd find everything imaginable—writings, sketches, notes, memorabilia, secrets, photos, and dreams.

It is this passion for note taking, making small sketches and adding a bit of color, along with my love of book making, that I share here. The journals in this book range from very simple embellished store-bought blank books to more complicated hand-sewn structures. But they are all designed to inspire you to begin one of your own and to fill it with your observations and experiences.

The Summertime Journal is super easy to make and can be adapted to capture the nuances of any season. Even easier, the Battle-of-Your-Life Journal is just a blank book you purchase and embellish, but I found making and keeping one to be a powerful tool in my fight against breast cancer. The very striking Hopelessly Sentimental Journal is actually a shoebox filled with plastic sleeves; it makes a wonderful repository for family memorabilia. And the Postcards Journal is unique and fun, yet making it requires little more than postcards and a hole punch.

If you've never made so much as a booklet before, don't worry. In the first chapter, I'll introduce you to the parts of a book, journal-making terms, and the tools and materials required. You can use this as an excuse to spend an afternoon roaming the aisles of a craft or art supply store, but you can also probably find many of the items you need tucked away in your desk or in a drawer in your kitchen.

The projects themselves give step-by-step instructions and use detailed illustrations to lead you through the making of the journals. Follow the steps to the letter or use them as inspiration and make your own version that suits your taste and needs. Make yours a different size, add more or fewer pages, or come up with your own unique way to decorate the cover. I've included glimpses of the inside pages of my journals, too, hoping that these will serve as inspiration when it comes time to use your journal.

The next chapter treats the word *journal* as a verb instead of a noun—it's all about using your journal. If you sometimes get blocked when you face a blank page, check out my pointers on how to jump in and start writing. If you haven't had an art class since grade school, you'll find my quick lesson on how to sketch and tips to get you started playing with color and paint useful. Don't be intimidated: capturing the silhouette of a landscape or a summer chair resting in a lavender field is really about observing closely. Carrying a journal or sketchbook is a journey in learning how to see.

My journals are also places of discovery. I have learned more about myself, about my passions, my likes and dislikes, what hurts me, and what makes me ecstatic because I journal. My journals are a comfort in difficult times. In moments of solitude and darkness, they are a place for fears, anxiety, reflection, and meditation. My life is richer because of journaling. I hope yours will be, too. I hope your world opens up and you fill the pages of your journals with ideas, dreams, and memories of your own.

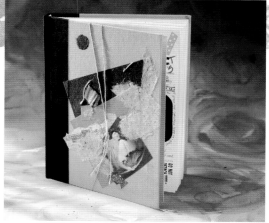

Battle-of-Your-Life Journal

Postcards Journal

Summertime Journal

Making & Embellishing Journals:
THE BASICS

Y ou don't have to be a Pulitzer Prize-winning author or skilled artist to keep a journal, and you don't need to be an expert bookmaker to make one. The projects in this book range from simply embellishing purchased notebooks to those requiring more complex bookbinding techniques. You can find one that matches your skill level or one that teaches you something new.

In the projects section, I explain the techniques for making and embellishing each specific journal with step-by-step instructions and illustrations. Projects repeat common techniques as needed, but you might find them easier to follow if you first familiarize yourself with the terms I use to describe the parts of a book.

Parts of a Book

Board: The board used as the front or back cover of the journal; it may be covered in paper or bookcloth or used as is.

Board Thickness: The thickness of the board material used as the cover. Sometimes a project calls for a measurement not in inches or millimeters, but simply in "board thicknesses."

Book Block: The total grouping of signatures or sheets that constitute the contents or body of a book. Also referred to as a text block.

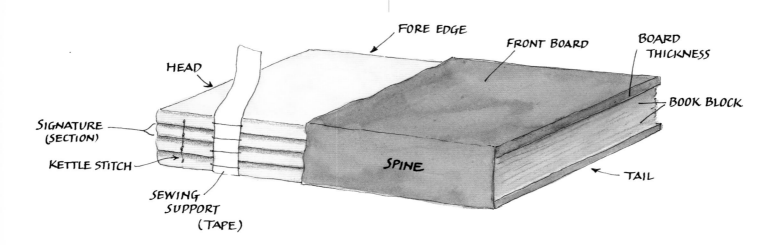

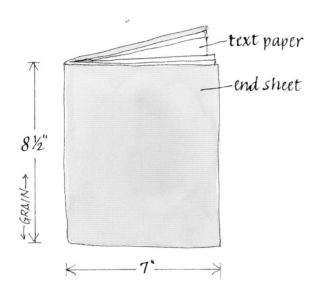

text paper

end sheet

8½"

GRAIN

7"

KETTLE STITCH

End Sheets: A folio or signature, often of decorative papers, placed at the inside of the front and back covers. End sheets are usually blank and may be of a different color or texture, but are always the same size as the other text pages.

Folio (not shown): A single sheet folded in half to create four pages, front and back.

Fore Edge: The opening front edge of a book, opposite the spine.

Front Board: See Board.

Head: The top of a book, folio, page, etc.

Kettle Stitch: A sewing stitch that links adjacent signatures securely together at the head and tail sewing stations.

Sewing Support: This is usually a ½- to ¾-inch-wide bookbinder's linen tape used to support the sewn structure, but in decorated journals it may be made of heavy-duty ribbon.

Signature: A gathering of folded sheets, sharing a common fold. Also called a section.

Spine: The backbone of a book. Structurally, it's the side that holds the book together.

Tail: The bottom of a book, folio, page, etc.

Journal-Making Terms

It will also be handy to know some of the terms used in the basic journal-making techniques that are covered in the project instructions. I've listed the key terms here.

Accordion Fold: A method of folding a sheet of paper, with alternating sections folding in a zigzig, fan-like structure, thus opening and closing like an accordion. It creates alternate mountain and valley folds in the paper.

Bone: To use the bone folder to press flat a crease in the paper. Also, to apply pressure to two pieces of material that have been glued together in order to smooth the surface and release trapped air bubbles.

Grain: The direction in which paper folds most easily, created by the direction of fibers in the papermaking process. Correct grain allows the pages to open more easily. Grain runs parallel to the line of least resistance; in a book, it runs from the head to the tail.

Hole Template: A piece of scrap paper, onto which you've marked the placement of holes to be punched or drilled into a cover, signature, and/or spine. Using a hole template ensures that the holes are made in the same place every time.

Mountain Fold: The peaked edge of paper that rises up, resembling a mountain on a folded sheet of paper, always between two valley folds.

MOUNTAIN AND VALLEY FOLDS

ACCORDION FOLD

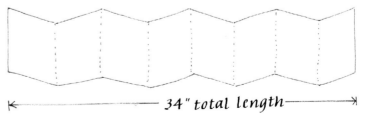

GRAIN → / ← GRAIN

6¼"

← 34" total length →

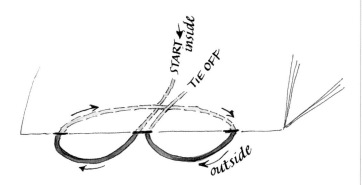

3-HOLE PAMPHLET STITCH

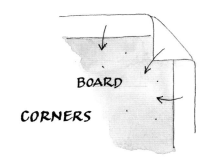

TURN-IN

Sewing: Many projects in this book call for some basic sewing. The most difficult part is threading the needle. If you can do that, you can complete these projects.

Square Knot: A basic knot for tying off thread. To tie one, remember this phrase: "Right over left, then left over right."

Three-Hole Pamphlet Stitch: An easy sewing technique to secure a three-hole perforated signature.

Turn-In: The extra allowances of covering material that are turned in over the edges of the cover boards of a book and glued in place.

Valley Fold: The creased indent that resembles a valley on a folded sheet of paper, always between two mountain folds.

Weaver's Knot: A type of knot used to connect two lengths of similar thread needed to lengthen the sewing thread.

Tools and Materials for Making and Embellishing Journals

Buy quality tools and materials and your journals will look better. In this section, I've defined a basic set of tools and materials you'll need to complete most of the projects in this book. You can find most of the items listed here in better art stores, crafts stores, bookbinding supply stores, or even hardware stores. When a project calls for you to embellish a journal, choose material that appeals to you—in color, texture, and weight.

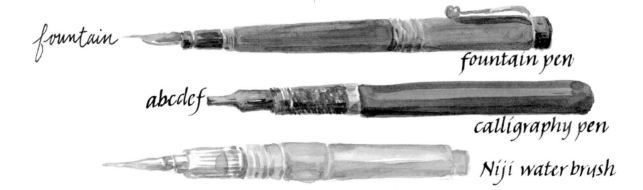

fountain

fountain pen

abcdef

calligraphy pen

Niji water brush

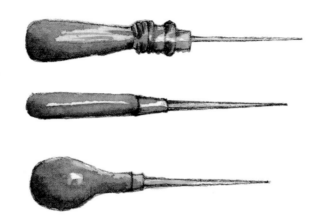

PIERCING TOOLS ~ AWL

Awl or Brad Awl: A straight, shafted awl for piercing holes or marking.

Beeswax: Beeswax often comes in handy for strengthening thread and keeping it from tangling when you're sewing. Apply conservatively.

Bone Folder: A flat, blunt instrument for scoring and folding paper, turning in corners, and smoothing out air bubbles on pasted surfaces. There are many varieties, but the most useful one has a pointed end and a blunt, rounded end.

Bookbinder's Boards: See Museum Boards.

Book Cloth: Paper-backed cloth sold by the yard from bookbinding suppliers. You can make your own by gluing a thin oriental paper to your choice of fabric.

BEESWAX

BONE FOLDER

Brushes: Besides watercolor brushes, you'll need brushes for applying glue. A stiff, blunt brush works best for applying PVA white glue, while a softer brush is needed for paste. You can find them at bookbinding suppliers or at craft stores.

Bulldog Clips: A heavy-duty clip used to hold a few signatures in position while you stitch or pierce. You can also use large paper clips or clothespins, but bulldog clips work best.

Craft Knife: A sharp knife found in craft stores that you use for making specialty cuts in paper. (Be sure to replace dull blades.) Used in conjunction with a cutting mat.

Cutting Mat: A self-healing mat used to protect work surfaces and to prevent craft knife blades from becoming dull too quickly. I recommend one that's 18 x 24 inches.

Glue Stick: For pasting your journals, I've found that acid-free glue works best.

Hole Punch: The one-hole punch called for in the projects throughout this book is a ¼-inch one. A good one can cut through most thicknesses of paper.

Metal Ruler: Besides being useful for taking measurements, a metal ruler works well with a bone folder for scoring paper to make precise folds. You can also use it as a straightedge in conjunction with a craft knife. I recommend one at least 18 inches long.

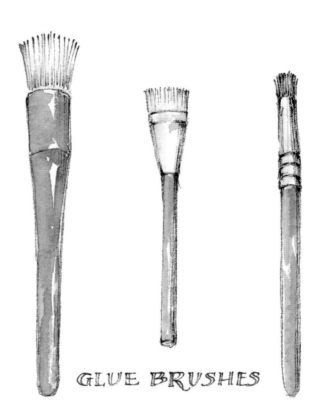

GLUE BRUSHES

ADHESIVES

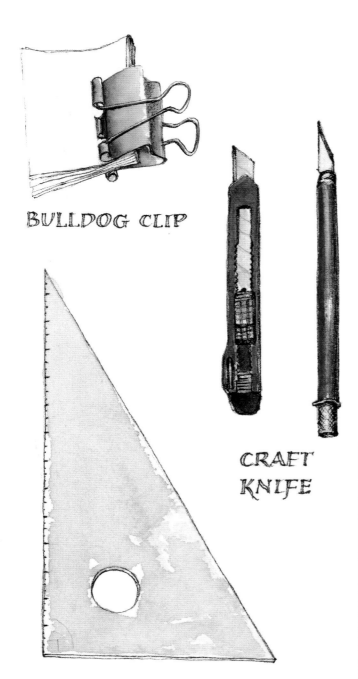

BULLDOG CLIP

CRAFT KNIFE

RIGHT ANGLE METAL TRIANGLE

Mini Bar Clamp: This kind of clamp locks to keep sections together while you drill or dry adhesives between pressing boards. You can also use C-clamps.

Museum Board: A 2- or 4-ply board used for book covers, it is also called conservation board. The most common type is book-binder's greyboard, which comes in a variety of weights and thicknesses. You can also use Bristol boards, illustration boards, or mat boards.

Needles: When you need to sew, I recommend using a book-binder's size 18 needle, but any large-eyed, blunt-ended needle will work.

Pencil: Any HB type will work fine. Don't forget a pencil sharpener.

Pressing Boards: Often used with weights, pressing boards help flatten covers and signatures. You can leave items between the boards anywhere from 15 minutes to overnight (or sometimes even longer, depending on the project).

PVA (Polyvinyl Acetate) Glue: A resinous adhesive that's also known as white glue or craft glue, PVA glue is easy to apply and can be thinned with water. The glue's characteristics (and acidity) vary depending on the brand. The best quality for bookbinding is flexible and pH neutral.

Right Triangle: When you have to draw a straight line perpendicular to an existing line or edge, use a right triangle or T-square. Purchase a metal one so you can also cut against it with a craft knife.

Scissors: Use scissors that are sharp. It often helps to have a smaller pair for cutting threads.

Small Hand Drill: For making holes in thicker boards or reams of paper. Be sure to place a scrap board underneath the project while drilling.

Thread: The best thread for strength is a bookbinder's linen thread, which is made from flax fiber. You can find it at a binding supplier. You can use buttonhole, upholsterer's thread, or carpet thread with beeswax. Threads noted for texture and decorative effects may not have the strength to sustain a project like binding thread. Thread must be strong enough to support a book, but not be so thin it cuts the pages.

Trim and Touch-Up Roller:
A 3-inch roller works best. Use it with a tray to distribute glue evenly and quickly on larger surfaces.

Waste Paper: When you need to keep work surfaces free from excess glue, use plain newsprint, magazine pages, junk mail, computer printout paper, or sheets of scrap paper.

Wax Paper: Wax paper acts as a moisture barrier between freshly glued sections and the other sections of a book, especially when you are pressing the book.

Weights: Anything heavy can serve as a weight, as long as it's stable. Use weights with pressing boards or for holding a book block in position while sewing multiple signatures.

SCISSORS

HAND DRILL

Papers

Using papers of various textures and colors will give your journals character. When choosing paper, consider its suitability to the inks, watercolor, glue, and other media you might use. Experiment. You can use a combination of paper varieties, adding artwork or lettering later. Some art supply stores offer sheet sample packets to help you decide. You'll find textured and smooth-finish papers, pure whites and creamy whites, thin text papers and thicker cover-weight sheets. I recommend using acid-free paper, which ensures the longevity of your work. Here are some paper types to consider:

Colored Paper Stock

There's a rainbow of colors to choose from when it comes to paper stock. Charcoal papers are excellent all-around drawing papers with a toothy surface that's ideal for pastels, soft pencils, and charcoal. Consider a section of colored paper in any handmade journal.

Graph Paper

Use the grid both vertically and horizontally to help with layout and placement. This paper is both visually interesting and a helpful drawing tool.

Oriental Paper

A versatile paper that's lightweight and soft yet strong. Oriental paper is often used as end sheets. You can also glue a lightweight oriental paper to your choice of fabric to create book cloth.

Scrapbook Paper

Check out the scrapbooking aisle in your local craft store, and you'll find a huge assortment of papers available for backgrounds or collages.

Tracing Paper

So useful in so many ways, tracing paper should be tucked into your travel journal for when you need a quick trace of something you can't take with you. This paper also comes in handy when transferring part of a sketch from one composition to another.

Watercolor Paper

If you have a travel watercolor kit or use watercolor pencils, watercolor paper is an excellent choice for pages in your journals since it can withstand being wet and is available in a variety of weights and finishes.

Keeping a Journal

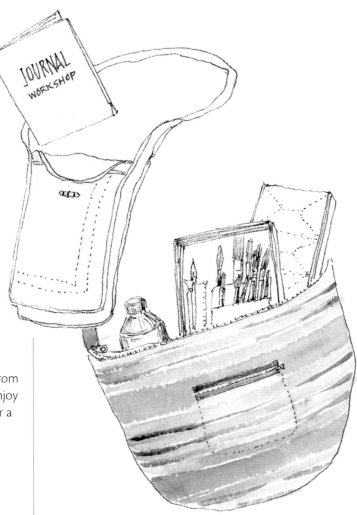

Making or embellishing a journal is a lot of fun. Getting started is pretty easy because you can read the list of materials and tools, gather your supplies, and then just follow the steps. Keeping a journal is also a lot of fun, but getting started can sometimes be a challenge. Perhaps you dream of a book filled with vivid, moving prose that captures your deepest thoughts on page after page of beautifully rendered sketches and paintings in striking color combinations. These grandiose expectations will keep you stuck in the dream stage, holding onto your blank journal until you've taken enough workshops to become an expert writer and illustrator.

I admire the carefree spirit who can plop down with a journal anywhere and everywhere, under all weather conditions, and knock out pages without rules. This kind of freedom comes from releasing your expectations and allowing yourself to simply enjoy the creative process. You don't need to be a talented writer or a skilled artist to keep a journal.

You just need to pick up a pen or pencil and get started.

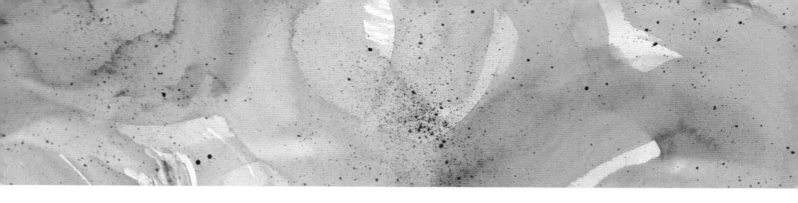

Words

Have you ever noticed how people are at their most eloquent when they're discussing a topic that stirs their passions? Well, the same is true for writing. Don't write about the things you think you ought to care about, write about what really gets you excited. If it's your favorite aunt's pie recipe, start there. Begin with the recipe, and then describe how the flakey crust melts in your mouth. The next thing you know, you may be recalling details of a special afternoon you spent in the kitchen together or the funny story she told you about how she met your uncle. Perhaps fishing is your passion. Consider a journal about a particular trip. Describe the lures and the weather conditions, the fish that got away and the ones you reeled in. Go ahead and embellish a bit—that's what fish stories are for.

This book is filled with suggested topics: nature; your family, friends, and pets; travel; memories and matters of the heart; and your health. Many people use their journals to record thoughts and experiences, but you can use yours as a support system, a way to capture those small glimmers of ideas. Once you have them down on paper, you can develop them later.

What's important is not how you write, but *that* you write. If you sit down to journal and suddenly feel the weight of a former English teacher or other critic perched on your shoulder, simply flick them off and write. Write like no one else will see your words. No one else has to.

Art

Using images to capture your thoughts and experiences can bring your journals to a whole new level. You don't need to be a trained artist to fill your pages with striking visuals. The journals in this book are decorated with photographs, rubber stamps, magazine clippings, maps, and even seed packets. Still, I would encourage you to try your hand at simple sketches and to play with paint just for the sheer joy of it.

SKETCHING AND DRAWING

Sketching and drawing are exercises in "seeing." Drawing well is a skill developed from both keen observation and a great deal of practice. You may not yet have the ability (or the time) to create elaborate and detailed drawings in the studio, but if you learn a few basic techniques, you can use sketching to enhance your journaling experience. Sketching captures an immediate impression and records it as an inspiration.

Sketching requires a quick focus to seize the present moment. When sketching in the field, the hand and mind must work together with speed to capture the dragonfly, the landscape from a moving car, or the view of vineyards. When you record the view before you, your intense focus links you to the scene; your hand records the transmitted energy.

Sketch wherever you can. Work on your ability to "see" and use any opportunity as an exercise. If you know you have only 10 minutes, then work quickly to get down the basic shapes, saving the details for last. Do thumbnail sketches, experimenting and sometimes altering the composition.

In sketching and drawing, there are four basic shapes—square, triangle, circle, and rectangle. When these shapes are given dimension and form, they become a cube, a cone, a ball, and a cylinder, respectively. In more complex arrangements, there are angles to consider and compare—for example, the distance from the corner of one object to the next. In your observations, notice the alignment between distant points as well as close ones.

When making a quick sketch for watercolor, lightly pencil the overall shapes. You can add a one-color swash of shading and values with a compact paint box. Make notes next to the sketch describing colors or other references. When drawing a fleeting image, develop a strong after-image vision and use a rapid sketching style. Learn to recognize and simplify the shapes you are seeing.

Have fun and be creative. Don't be afraid to make marks on a blank page. Observe things from a different point of view. Communicate the colors of a sunset or flowers with words or visuals. Collage other ideas with images to capture a scene, a feeling, or a memory.

Drawing Exercise: Draw a Coffee Mug

Materials:

Coffee mug with handle
Paper
Pencil

1 Observe a single subject—a coffee mug in this example. Instead of concentrating on what the object is, visualize the shapes that comprise its form.

2 The view before you is three-dimensional; the paper is two. Therein lies the problem. It's sometimes easier to draw from a photo because it, like your paper, is two-dimensional. Look at the coffee mug as if you were viewing it through a windowpane. The glass in the window serves as a two-dimensional plane. You've just reduced the mug to two dimensions.

3 The drawing technique is based on measuring the relationship of one line or form next to another. Using the pencil as a "sighting stick," hold your arm outstretched, elbow locked and pencil in hand. Grasp the pencil with four fingers and use the tip of your

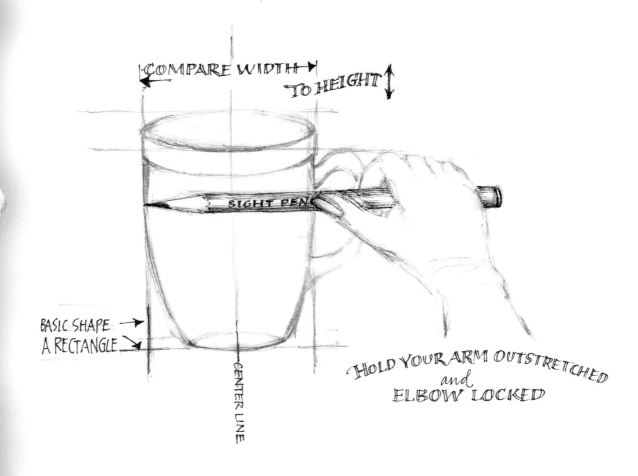

COMPARE WIDTH TO HEIGHT

SIGHT PENC

BASIC SHAPE
A RECTANGLE

CENTER LINE

HOLD YOUR ARM OUTSTRETCHED
and
ELBOW LOCKED

thumb to hold the place of measurement. Keep your elbow locked or the measurements will differ. Also, make sure the pencil stays in alignment with the "glass picture plane" and not tilted, pointing towards or away from the object. Now, sighting with the pencil, compare the width of the coffee mug to its height. Whichever is the shortest distance, use it as the root unit of measure. Record height and width lines, and note if it forms a square or rectangle.

4 Sight and notice the difference in measurements between the width of the mug and the width of the handle. Continue with comparisons. Notice the depth of the ellipse at the opening of the cup rim in comparison to some other part on the cup. For example, compare the ellipse distance to the area where the handle attaches.

5 The "inner" negative space of the handle creates a shape. Instead of focusing on the actual handle and drawing that, focus on the negative shape. Let your eyes divert back and forth as you draw. Continue sketching with light to medium pressure. Readjust the marks on the page without erasing. You can make a more confident, definitive line on top of the sketching lines when you're finished.

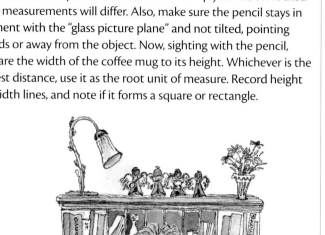

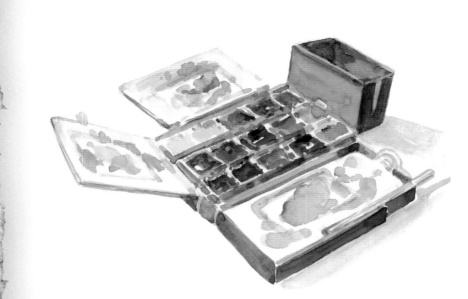

Watercolor Tips

Use high-quality paper, brushes, and paint for the highest quality results. Thicker paper buckles less than thin paper. Use a sample page to test colors before painting to avoid unwanted (and unalterable) effects, or you can experiment in the side margins of your journal pages.

Using a pencil and gummy eraser, sketch onto the watercolor paper. Use a light touch, and then erase the darker lines. Note how the light reflects from its source. The white of the paper serves as the pure white parts of your painting (or the highlights), so don't paint over all of it.

You can use watercolors straight from the tube or cake. They're also designed to be mixed—and the variations are endless. Use large containers (such as large plastic yogurt containers) of clean, clear water, and change it often. A double-rinse system is ideal: one for the initial dirty wash and another for the final, clear rinse.

Start with the lightest washes of color, and build up the intensity by layering washes on top of one another. Build from light to dark. Lay a colored wash over paint that's already dry. Experiment! Other techniques include painting wet-into-wet or mixing the paint directly on the page. Use a hairdryer if you're impatient, or a handheld mini travel fan.

To lift color, clean a brush with clear water, then squeeze most of the moisture out of it. (The brush must have less water than the surface of the paper.) Use the tip of the brush to loosen any dry pigment and then blot with tissue paper. For more aggressive removal, use a moistened stiff-bristled brush to gently "scrub" the area and then blot it with a tissue.

ADDING COLOR

Color is the most fundamental ingredient of visual communication. It can be intense, bright, subdued, or diluted. The study of color and the art of painting require a lot of hard work and "time behind the brush." But that doesn't mean you should shy away from using paint or watercolor to add color to your pages.

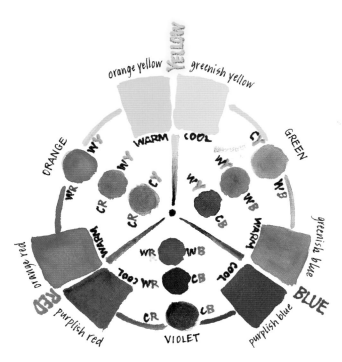

TWO - COLOR PRIMARY SYSTEM

As you can tell from the illustrations in this book, I love using watercolors to express myself. I've found it to be a wonderful tool for journaling. It's a spontaneous, fresh medium that is quick drying and easy to pack up to move to the next location. All it requires, besides the paint itself, is water, brushes, and some paper. If you'd like to become proficient at watercolor, enroll in a class or study books on the topic and just roll up your sleeves and jump in. Meanwhile, there's no reason you can't experiment with the medium to enhance your journals. The tips that follow will help get you started.

Mixing Colors

Putting a wet brush into the paint box to find an exact color match can be frustrating, confusing, and intimidating. You may be tempted to purchase every color because you can't produce the color you're seeking with the typical primary color triad of red, yellow, and blue. Instead, I recommend selecting a palette of two slightly different hues of each of the three primary colors—this is called a Two-Color Primary System.

Y = YELLOW
R = RED
B = BLUE
C = COOL
W = WARM

- COLORS ADJACENT ON COLOR WHEEL ARE BRIGHTER WHEN COMBINED.
- COMBINATIONS IN CENTER MOVE TO DARKER DOT, DULLER

The color spectrum is divided into warm and cool colors. Generally, we think of red, yellow, and orange as warm colors, and blue, green, and violet as cool colors; however, if you place two different reds side by side, such as Cadmium Red and Alizarin Crimson, you can see the variation in the pigment temperature. Cadmium Red appears warmer as it has a little yellow in it, while Alizarin Crimson appears cooler as it has a little blue in it. When choosing your two reds, yellows, and blues, make sure one of each is warm and one is cool.

For my limited basic travel palette, I use Aureolin Yellow, Alizarin Crimson, and Cerulean Blue for cool colors, and Cadmium Yellow, Cadmium Red, and French Ultramarine Blue for warm colors. For additional pigments, I also use Burnt Umber, Viridian, Winsor Violet, and Yellow Ochre. You may prefer to substitute other colors, depending on your subject matter.

To find a color's complement, look for the opposite color on the primary color wheel (see the chart to the right). The complement of blue, for example, is simply a mixture of the remaining two primaries—red and yellow (or orange). When you mix two opposite colors they neutralize each other and produce rich unusual color combinations. In this case, the color created by mixing blue and orange is a beautiful warm gray, perfect for shading blues and oranges. Mix complements in different proportions to create rich varieties of tones and note the remarkable range of colors you can make.

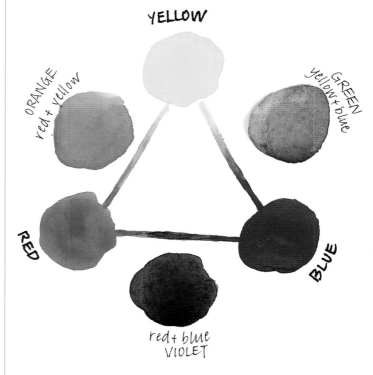

YELLOW

ORANGE
red + yellow

GREEN
yellow + blue

RED

BLUE

red + blue
VIOLET

COLOR WHEEL

AUREOLIN YELLOW CADMIUM YELLOW ALIZARIN CRIMSON

CERULEAN BLUE ULTRAM. BLUE CADMIUM RED

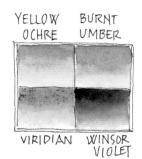

YELLOW OCHRE BURNT UMBER

VIRIDIAN WINSOR VIOLET

With practice, you can learn to create intense or subdued color with a Double Primary Palette. Intensity of a color, sometimes called saturation, is its brightness or dullness. For example, to create green you mix yellow and blue, but to create a bright intense green you can mix Cerulean Blue, which leans towards yellow, and Aureolin Yellow, which leans towards blue. Yellowish blue and bluish yellow create a bright green. If you use Cadmium Yellow, which leans towards red (and red is the complement, or opposite, of green), you'll compromise, or dull, the brilliancy of the green, thus lowering its intensity.

COMPLEMENTS are opposites on the color wheel
and produce lively neutrals – grays & browns

Tools for Journaling

Sometimes having the perfect pen can really make me want to write. It's the same, of course, with drawing and painting implements. Familiarize yourself with journaling tools by making marks with them—in your journals. Allow the journal page to be your scratch pad. Include the name of the tool, brand, size, etc. Each tool has a special quality and will respond differently depending on the feel and pressure of your hand. Good line quality, fluidity of movement, and nice textural paper are all qualities that contribute a "happiness factor" to the journaling process. Don't be afraid to experiment.

The tonal palette of pencil leads ranges from dark to light. A "B" code indicates a dark/soft lead; an "H" code indicates a light/hard lead. A "B" pencil is good for sketching, but "HB" lead is useful for a preliminary sketch that you will paint over. A small hand-held pencil sharpener or a good sharp craft knife is a must. My choice for an eraser is a white plastic eraser or a kneaded rubber eraser.

Colored pencils are great for color notes. A good-quality pencil contains more pigment than the student-grade variety. You can also use watercolor pencils that become liquid color when you apply a wet brush—they're great for creating in the field.

pencil sharpener

eraser

great ideas

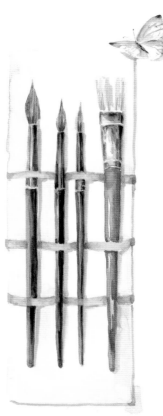

fine-line Pens

pen nibs

Brushes

Keep a variety of pens. A fine-line waterproof pigment liner is also lightfast. My favorites are a fine-line 01 and a micron 005. The micro roller-ball pen makes a very fluid line. My favorite writing tool is the fountain pen. I enjoy seeing the wet ink as I'm writing, even though it's momentary. I enjoy the tactile quality of the nib as it glides across the paper, and a wet brush can pull out tonal effects in the sketch.

Use good brushes. While sable brushes are best, they can be costly. A good sable blend or good-quality synthetic works just fine. The three sizes to have are no. 2 (for fine details), no. 4, and no. 8 (for general use). You can fill in larger areas with a ¾ inch flat brush. Use only watercolor brushes for watercolors, and take care of them. Rinse the brush well in clean water after use and reshape the end with your fingers. A white cotton cloth can tell you if leftover pigment remains in the brush. Never let your brushes sit in water. I recommend you make a brush holder so the hairs don't get damaged in transit.

A watercolor traveling paint box is compact, light, and convenient for painting on the road. A small paint box can contain half pans of paint or your choice of tubes, which you can squeeze into small palette sections as needed. In either case, buy the best quality artists' paints you can afford, as student-grade colors tend to contain less pigment and lack the vibrancy of artist-grade watercolors.

Masking fluid, which you apply with a synthetic brush, creates a waterproof film on the page that protects whatever area you want to mask—usually the white areas on the page that can get lost. When the painted area is dry, you can remove the masking fluid with a rubber cement pick up.

You'll need a small open-mouthed jar with a lid for water. I also have a larger, portable water container that folds flat. Remember to use plenty of clean water and to change it frequently to keep your colors fresh.

I've found that a small natural sea sponge is useful for putting on color, removing color, and cleaning up. Keep it clean!

You'll get the most use out of your journal if you can use it whenever and wherever inspiration hits. Easy accessibility to paints, brushes, pencils, and the book itself makes the journaling process simple to do at a moment's notice. Set-up should not be a burden. You'll need writing, sketching, and/or painting tools that travel well and some type of bag or backpack to keep everything close at hand. The bag is as important a tool to a journal keeper as a camera bag is to a photographer.

Rubber cement pick-up

Masking Fluid

Water Jar

Natural sponge

NEVER own more than
you can fit in a BACKPACK

TAKAHASHI

Chapter 1

SEASONS

Each season has its own spell. Journaling is a wonderful way to slow yourself down so you stop and observe the changing seasons. Notice the color palette of the particular time of year—the pastel hues in the buds and blossoms of spring, the intense, bursting colors of summer, the cast of golden tones in autumn, and the beautiful silhouettes of trees in winter. Feel the seasonal light and the changes in temperature and humidity. Being fully aware of the seasons wherever you are—whether surrounded by nature or in the city—makes you feel more alive and a part of all that's around you.

Summertime Journal

This single-signature pamphlet is the simplest and most basic journal structure. Consider devoting one journal to each season. When it starts, allow the pages to absorb the essence of its days. I've chosen summer because its warm months have always led to fond memories.

What You Need

Oilcloth, 8½" x 30" (for the cover)

Pencil

PVA glue

Bone folder

Wax paper

2 pressing boards, with weights

4 sheets of text paper, 8½" x 14"

1 sheet of lightweight decorative paper, 8½" x 14"

1 sheet of scrap paper for template (at least 8½" long)

4 large paper clips

Awl

Bookbinding needle or large-eye needle

Heavy thread, at least 21¼" long

Scissors

Small beads (optional)

What You Do

To Make the Cover:

1 On the wrong side of the oilcloth, mark the centerfold line and the two fore edge fold lines (see diagram A). In other words, divide the cloth into four equal lengths, 7½" each.

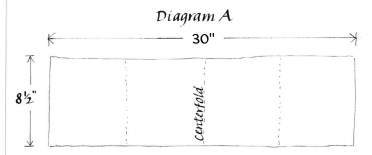

Diagram A

2 Add glue to the wrong side of the oilcloth, on the far right-hand quarter. Fold along the fore edge fold line to the center. Apply the bone folder to smooth the crease. This is the back cover.

3 Repeat step 2 to create the front cover, gluing the far left-hand quarter.

4 With the sheet of wax paper between the front and back covers, fold it closed. Place between the two pressing boards, under weights, for 15 minutes.

To Make the Text Pages:

5 Wrap the lightweight decorative paper around the four sheets of text paper as an end sheet, and fold in half to create one signature (see diagram B).

Diagram B

—text paper

—end sheet

8½"

GRAIN→

7"

6 Make a four-hole template from the piece of scrap paper (see diagram C). Mark holes 1 and 4, ½" from the head and tail, respectively. Mark holes 2 and 3 equidistant from holes 1 and 4.

Diagram C

hole template

7 Place the template on the opened signature within the cover (see diagram C again); secure with the large paper clips. With the awl, pierce sewing holes through the sheets and the cover. Remove the hole template, leaving the paper clips in place.

8 Thread the needle with thread that's two and a half times the length of the spine. Begin sewing from outside hole 2 (see diagram D), leaving 5" of loose thread.

enter

hole 1
hole 2
hole 3
hole 4

Diagram D

9 Proceed along the inside of the spine and exit hole 3. Enter hole 4, then loop back to exit hole 3, pulling the thread taut. Proceed along the outer spine to enter hole 1. Loop back to exit hole 2, where you started. Your stitches should be tight enough to hold the journal together without preventing it from easily closing.

10 Tie a square knot with the thread from step 8.

11 Optional. String the small beads onto the thread to create a decorative tassel for your journal. Tie another square knot to hold the beads in place.

What's Inside

The summertime page was done with a splash of gouache watercolors. The list of "favorite things" was lettered in brush, and the writing was done with a fine-line pen.

Gardening Journal

Opening the cover of a gardening journal is like stepping through a gate and into a garden. Of course, gardens come in all sizes and styles—some are peaceful and have a calming effect, while others are filled with flowers of bursting brilliant color and surprising wild beauty.

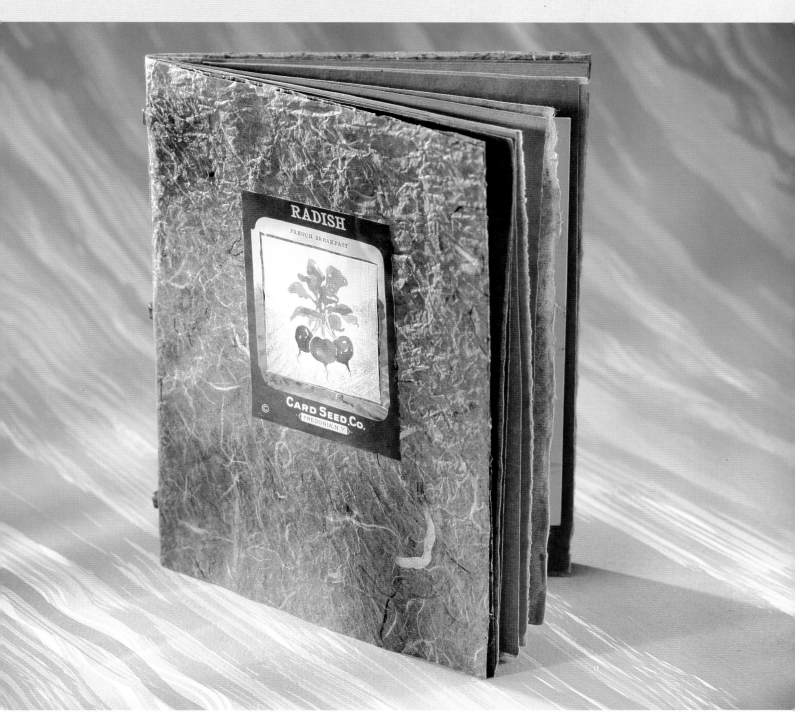

What You Need

Heavyweight decorative paper,
9½" x 16½" (for cover)

Metal ruler

Bone folder

6 sheets of bond paper, 9" x 13½"
(for text pages)

Scrap paper, about 2" x 10"
(for hole template)

Scissors

Pencil

Large paper clips

Awl

Needle and thread (or yarn)

3 decorative beads

What You Do

1 Pleat the heavyweight paper to make a mountain fold, as
shown in diagram A. Apply the bone folder to the creases.

Diagram A

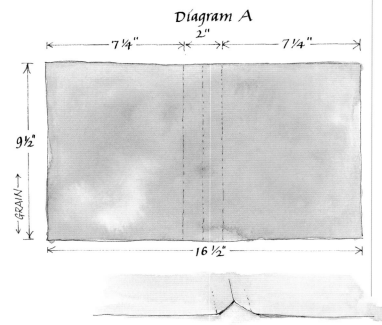

Pleated Cover

2 Fold the sheets of the bond paper to create two signatures of
three sheets each (see diagram B). Each page should measure
9" x 6¾". Apply the bone folder to the creases.

Diagram B

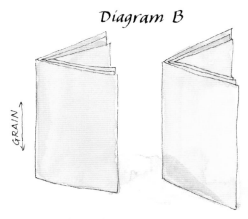

two signatures ~
three sheets each

3 Open the two signatures and align their center folds with the
valley folds of the cover's pleat (see diagram C). The cover
should be right sides (i.e., good sides) together.

Diagram C
Cover - right sides
together

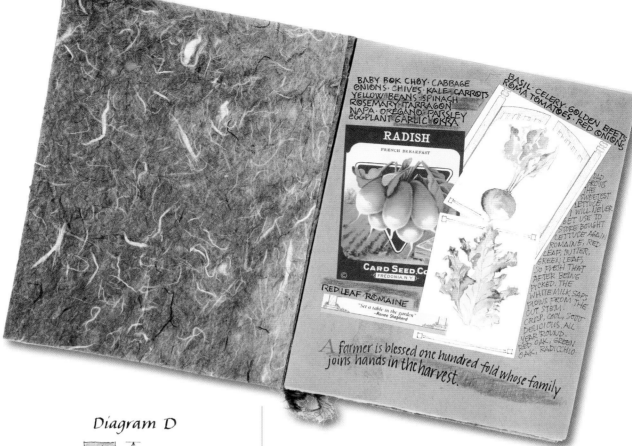

BABY BOK CHOY · CABBAGE
ONIONS · CHIVES · KALE · CARROTS
YELLOW BEANS · SPINACH
ROSEMARY · TARRAGON
NAPA · OREGANO · PARSLEY
EGGPLANT GARLIC OKRA

BASIL · CELERY · GOLDEN BEETS
ROMA TOMATOES · RED ONIONS

RADISH

FRENCH BREAKFAST

CARD SEED CO.
FREDONIA, N.Y.

RED LEAF ROMAINE

"Set a table in the garden"
—Renee Shepherd

HAD
GROWN
THE
SWEETEST
LETTUCE.
WILL NEVER
GET USE TO
STORE BOUGHT
LETTUCE AGAIN.
ROMAINE, RED
LEAF, BUTTER,
GREEN LEAF.
SO FRESH THAT
AFTER BEING
PICKED, THE
WHITE MILK SAP
FLOWS FROM THE
CUT STEM.
CRISP, COOL, SCOUT
DELICIOUS. ALL
YEAR ROUND.
RED OAK, GREEN
OAK, RADICCHIO.

A farmer is blessed one hundred fold whose family
joins hands in the harvest.

Diagram D

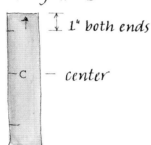

↕ 1" both ends

— C — center

3-hole template

4 To create the three-hole template, cut the scrap paper to the height of the cover (9½"). Along one side, mark 1" from the top and bottom. Fold the template in half lengthwise to find the center point; mark that too (see diagram D).

5 Lay the template in the center of the top signature and secure with the paper clips, making sure both signatures are aligned (see diagram E). With the awl, pierce holes through both signatures and the cover paper as one unit.

Diagram E

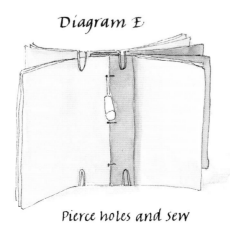

Pierce holes and sew

Diagram F

Start
End → tie off

6 Sew a three-hole pamphlet stitch through the entire unit, catching a bead within the cover spine pleat—in the center of the bundle—at each sewing station (see diagram F). Tie off the two ends of thread.

41

Today I have witnessed nature's wonder. The birth of a poppy blossom from its green hairy cocoon pod. The pod first burst from the base releasing the bi-valve pod upwards, still attached - hinged at the top.

The flower remained in a pointed brush shape - STILL. The petals were crinkled tight like an umbrella that hadn't been opened a whole season or like my down sleeping bag scrunched into a miniature nylon sack. Petals like delicate paper-silk. The stamens lay neatly in the bowl, not yet flexing forth.

What's Inside

The inside pages of the Gardening Journal are charcoal papers that have been color-stained to give them a weathered, earthy feel. The opening page (see page 41) features a seed packet and watercolors of vegetables. I included a list of some vegetables grown on our farm. Here, a watercolor of a poppy spotted in the field accompanies an entry about the event. The page is stitched onto the folded center spine with decorative yarn.

What to Include

- Lists of dream gardens, plants, landscaping ideas, garden furniture.

- A garden map.

- Garden visitors: pets, butterflies, bees, birds.

- Names of plants, herbs, and flowers in the garden and their characteristics you love.

- Record of seasonal tasks: sowing, weeding, pruning, staking, planting bulbs, harvesting.

- Vegetable gardens: times to harvest and recipes that result from the harvest.

- Weather: rainfall, sun, wind, and dates of first and last frosts.

Nature-Watching Journal

I learned to use a field guide many years ago when I first began to notice the variety of birds along the seashore. This project uses a simple accordion structure that allows you to view one entry or several entries at the same time. Use as many pages as you need to record your nature notes and sketches.

What You Need

12 sheets of bond paper, 7¼" x 7"

Nature log template (see page 125)

Shoebox lid

PVA glue

Glue brush

2 sheets of scrap paper (waste sheets for gluing), one 8" x 8" and one 8" x 1"

2 pressing boards, with weights

Metal ruler

Scissors

Book cloth strip for spine, 1¼" x 8½"

Pencil

Card stock strip for spine, ³⁄₁₆" x 7½"

2 pieces of 4-ply board, 3⅝" x 7½", available at good art stores

Bone folder

1 strip of decorative paper, 1¼" x 7¼"

2 larger pieces of decorative paper, 4⅛" x 8½"

2 smaller pieces of decorative paper, 3⅜" x 7¼"

Wax paper

What You Do

To Make the Accordion:

1 If desired, copy the nature log template onto the bond paper. Fold all the sheets of bond paper in half lengthwise (into 7¼" x 3½" size). Place the first sheet into the shoebox lid with its head and spine against the inside of the box lid (see diagram A).

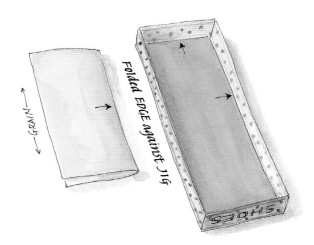

Diagram A

2 Unfold the second sheet and apply glue to the right edge, using the method shown in diagram B.

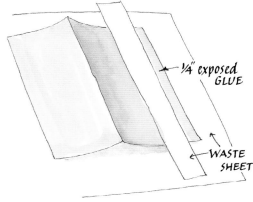

Diagram B

3 Place the sheet into the shoe box jig, folded with the glue side down, on top of the first sheet with the spines and heads aligned. Repeat with the rest of the sheets.

4 Take all the glued sheets out of the shoebox and place them between the pressing boards, under weights, for at least 30 minutes.

5 Open the accordion fold—all the glued sheets together—as shown in diagram C. Trim ¼" bevels on the last folio. Then cut the last folio, as shown, to create a 1" tab. Trim any uneven edges at the head and fore edge as necessary.

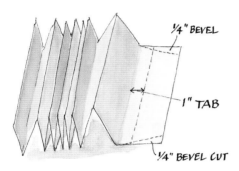

¼" BEVEL

1" TAB

¼" BEVEL CUT

Diagram C

To Create the Cover:

6 On the 1¼" x 8½" strip of book cloth, draw one line ½" from the top and another ½" from the bottom edge (see diagram D).

BOOKCLOTH

1¼"

Diagram D

7 Glue the 4-ply board and the card stock strip to the wrong side of the book cloth (see diagram E). Fold over the ½" turnover ends of the book cloth and glue in place. Apply the bone folder to smooth all glued surfaces.

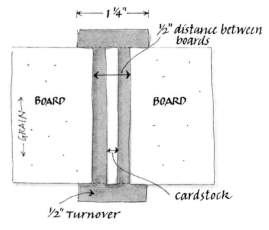

1¼"

½" distance between boards

GRAIN

BOARD

BOARD

cardstock

½" Turnover

Diagram E

8 Glue the strip of decorative paper to the inside spine, leaving ¼" of space at the head and tail (see diagram F). Apply the bone folder.

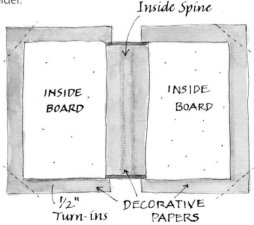

Inside Spine

INSIDE BOARD

INSIDE BOARD

½" Turn-ins

DECORATIVE PAPERS

Diagram F

9 Place the larger pieces of decorative paper underneath the fronts of the 4-ply boards with ½" turn-ins on three sides (see diagram F again). Glue the first piece to the outside of the front board. Apply the bone folder.

10 Trim the paper corners at a 45° angle, about ¼" (1½ board thicknesses) from the corner (see diagram G).

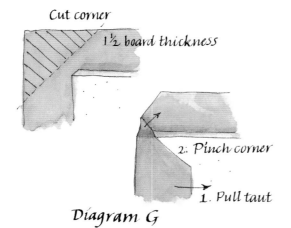

Cut corner

1½ board thickness

2. Pinch corner

1. Pull taut

Diagram G

11 Turn in and glue the head and tail ends of the paper first and then the fore edge. Gently pull the paper taut, making sure the edges adhere to the board. Be sure to pinch the paper over the corner using the bone folder (see diagram G again). Repeat steps 10 and 11 with the back cover.

To Connect the Text Block:

12 Rest the accordion against the book's spine (see diagram H) and glue the text block's 1" tab to the inside of the back cover. Paste the smaller pieces of decorative paper inside the back and front covers, ⅛" from the head, tail, and fore edge.

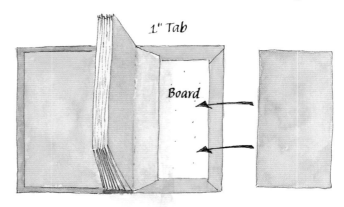

1" Tab

Board

Diagram H

13 Wrap the entire text block in wax paper. Wax paper acts as a moisture barrier between the freshly glued book covers and the text pages.

14 Press the journal between boards overnight.

Artist's Touch
To Bind or Not

This journal is made with loose sheets folded in half and glued at the fore edges. It's a great binding if you have loose pages. You can turn the pages one by one (like a book) or you can view all the pages at the same time (like an accordion) by pulling the text block out of the covers.

What's Inside

The inside end papers are oriental grass papers.
I did the nature-watching entries with various
pens, including a calligraphy fountain pen and
a fine-line 01 pen. I made the color notes in
colored pencil.

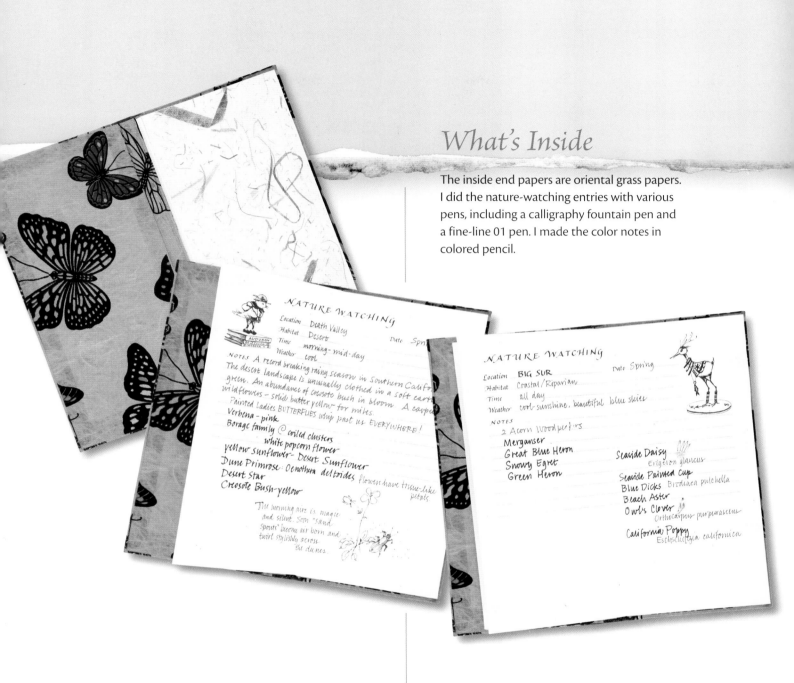

NATURE WATCHING

Location Death Valley
Habitat Desert   Date Spr...
Time morning- mid-day
Weather cool

NOTES A record breaking rainy season in Southern Califor...
The desert landscape is unusually clothed in a soft earth...
green. An abundance of creosote bush in bloom. A carpe...
wildflowers – solid butter yellow- for miles.
    Painted Ladies BUTTERFLIES whip past us EVERYWHERE!
Verbena – pink
Borage family @ coiled clusters
            white popcorn flower
Yellow Sunflower- Desert Sunflower
Dune Primrose- Oenothera deltoides flowers have tissue-like
Desert Star   petals
Creosote Bush-yellow

    The morning air is magic
    and silent. Soft "sand
    spouts" become air born and
    twirl stylishly across
        the dunes.

NATURE WATCHING

Location BIG SUR   Date Spring
Habitat Coastal / Riparian
Time all day
Weather cool-sunshine, beautiful blue skies

NOTES
    2 Acorn Woodpeckers
Merganser
Great Blue Heron
Snowy Egret   Seaside Daisy
Green Heron   Erigeron glaucus
                            Seaside Painted Cup
                            Blue Dicks Brodiaea pulchella
                            Beach Aster
                            Owl's Clover
                                Orthocarpus purpurascens
                            California Poppy
                                Eschscholtzia californica

12" Rainbow Trout - north fork of Yuba River. The Lure, Downieville, California ... lunch

Chapter 2

PASSIONS

When you feel passionate about something, it's easy to write about it. The journals in this chapter record my love of scrapbooking, cooking, and bookbinding. You may decide to create a journal that focuses on a different topic—any hobby, sport, or other activity that brings you pleasure. What counts is not the subject matter but putting your whole heart into the keeping of your journal. Time is well spent when you're doing that which you love most.

Scrapbooking Journal

Journaling is a wonderful addition to scrapbooking. This scrapbooking journal features a page with photo windows that let you highlight areas of a photograph. The page also has a wheel card that spins to reveal small photos or pieces of artwork.

What You Need

2 pieces of white card stock, each 8½" x 11"

Craft knife

Cutting mat

Metal ruler

Photos

Tracing paper

Removable tape

Fine-line marker

Pencil

Scrapbook or journal of your choice

Awl

Photo tape

Writing pen

Decorative paper or extra scrapbook page

Double-sided tape

Wheel and window templates (page 52)

Access to a photocopier (optional; see step 9)

Scissors

6 small photographs or pieces of art

Mini brad with a flat head

What You Do

To Make the Photo Windows:

1 Using the cutting mat, the craft knife, and the metal ruler, cut one piece of card stock into two 1½" x 8½" L-shaped pieces to create an adjustable mat-cropping frame (see diagram A).

Diagram A

11"

8½"

Cut out rectangle

Cut lines

"L" FRAMES

2 Lay a piece of the tracing paper over the first photo, tape the paper down with the removable tape, and use the fine-line marker to trace around the perimeter of the photo.

3 Use the mat-cropping frame to decide which sections of the photograph you want to highlight by cropping. When you've framed a desired area, make a light pencil mark on the tracing paper at each inside corner of the frame.

4 Use the pencil and the ruler to draw straight lines connecting the crop marks. Repeat steps 3 and 4 for each crop you want to make for that photo (see the example below).

5 To transfer the marks to the album page, place the tracing paper on the photo album page where you want the photo. Secure it with the removable tape and then put the cutting mat beneath the page. With the awl, pierce each corner of the photo crop rectangles; then remove the tracing paper.

6 Using the pierced marks as a guide, cut out the windows with the craft knife and metal ruler. Place the photograph behind the window and secure it with photo tape.

7 Use the writing pen to journal in the area surrounding the exposed photographs (see the example below).

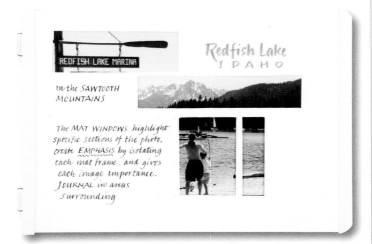

8 Use a sheet of the decorative paper or a sheet from the scrapbook as a backing for this page. Secure it to the page with the double-sided tape.

To Make the Wheel Card Page:

9 Use the template on page 125 to trace and cut out a wheel from the second piece of card stock. Optionally, you can enlarge or reduce the wheel template with a photocopier.

10 Cut the six photos or artwork just slightly larger than the bold shapes on the wheel. They don't have to be exactly the same size; the window on the scrapbook page through which they'll appear acts as a mat. Use the photo tape to secure the photos or artwork in place, and write a brief caption over each one.

11 Decide where you want to position the wheel behind the scrapbook page—just be sure to place the wheel so that part of its outer edge touches the top edge of the page.

12 Use the tracing paper and the pencil to transfer the template for the windows onto the scrapbook page. The top window exposes the caption and the edge of the wheel, so it's easy to turn. The bottom window shows the photos or artwork.

13 Use the craft knife to cut the window out of the scrapbook page. Use the mini flat brad to anchor the photo wheel to the scrapbook page. (A flat brad won't dent the pages that lie on top.)

Artist's Touch

A Few Scrapbooking Tips

The lettering for names, quotes, and titles can be made with a computer and printer, rubber stamps, or by hand. Never use paper made from wood pulp in your scrapbooks or journals—this type of paper has a high acidity content, which makes it difficult to preserve. Use papers, tapes, and inks that are of archival quality, pH-balanced, and as free from chemical impurities as possible. The inkpads, calligraphy pens, fine-line markers, and inks you use should be acid-free, permanent, and waterproof.

Cooking Journal

Indulge your love of cooking by creating a journal in which you record special recipes and mealtime memories. Keep track of ritual dishes—from fancy, special-occasion entrées to the quick dinners you whip up every week. Include photos of special meals and table settings, and add captions.

What You Need

Tea towel (or other fabric for front cover)

Fabric scissors

3 2-ply boards, each 6¼" x 4¼"

PVA glue

Bone folder

Book cloth

2 pressing boards, with weights

Craft knife and cutting mat

Scissors

Pencil

Hand drill with ¹⁄₁₆" bit

Index cards, 4" x 6"

2 loose-leaf rings, each ¾"

What You Do

To Cover the Front Board:

1 Cut the tea towel to the size of the 2-ply boards plus a ¾" margin on all sides (7 ¾" x 5 ¾").

2 Place the tea towel right side down. Position a 2-ply board in the center of the towel (see diagram A). Because the towel might fray at the corners if cut, make library miters by folding one corner at a 45° angle over the board corner (see diagram B). Gently pull the fabric taut and glue it down. Repeat at all corners. Then fold the ¾" margins up and over each covered corner, pull them snug, and glue them down. Apply the bone folder to the edges to get rid of any bubbles.

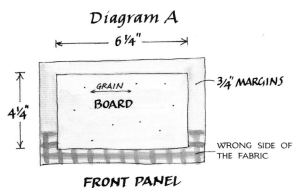

Diagram A

GRAIN
BOARD
6¼"
4¼"
¾" MARGINS
WRONG SIDE OF THE FABRIC

FRONT PANEL

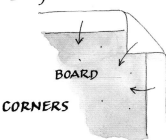

Diagram B

BOARD

CORNERS

3 To cover the inside of the front cover, cut a rectangle of book cloth slightly smaller than the board (¾" all around or 6" x 4") and glue it to the inside cover. Place the cover between the pressing boards and under weights for 15 minutes.

To Cover the Back Panels:

4 Cut one of the other 2-ply boards so that it measures 6¼" x 2½".

5 Cut the book cloth into an 8½" x 7¾" rectangle. Set the book cloth right side down and then place the 2-ply boards on top, arranged as shown in diagram C. Draw on the wrong side of the cloth to show the placement of the boards.

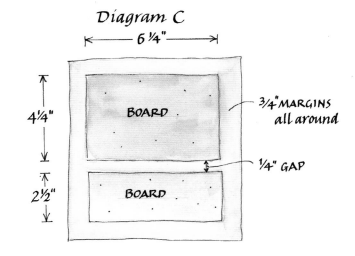

Diagram C

6¼"
4¼"
BOARD
¾" MARGINS all around
¼" GAP
2½"
BOARD

BACK PANELS

6 Apply glue to the wrong side of the cloth, and set both boards in place. Turn the cloth over and apply the bone folder to smooth all glued surfaces.

7 To create mitered corners, cut each book cloth corner at a 45° angle, 1½ board thicknesses from the board (see diagram D). Put glue on the margins, fold them over, and then smooth them with the bone folder. Press the corner with the tip of the bone folder to make sure it adheres well. Repeat for all corners.

Diagram D

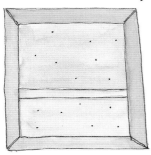

1½ board thicknesses away

BOARD

8 Cut the book cloth for the inside back so that it's slightly smaller than the back panel section (⅛" all around or 6 ¾" x 6"). See diagram E. Glue the book cloth down; then apply the bone folder, especially in the ¼" groove. Place the cover between pressing boards, under weights, with the flap in a closed position, for 15 minutes.

Diagram E

INSIDE BOOKCLOTH

To Drill Holes in the Covers:

9 Use the hand drill to make two holes at the top of the covers and all the index cards (see diagram F). Drill the holes 1⅜" from the sides and ⅜" from the top.

Diagram F

1⅜" from each end

⅜" from edge

HOLE PLACEMENT

10 Place the index cards between the covers; then add the loose-leaf rings. The journal should lie flat when closed and tented when open (see diagrams G and H).

Diagram G

Diagram H

DAMES apple strudel

The DAMES - that is one group that can really put out a "spread". This was served at a brunch fundraiser for the symphony. Served with cheese - Stilton. Gracie delivered the recipe as a gift tucked inside a basket with STRUDEL!

½ lb. filo dough
½ c. melted butter
4 tart cooking apples, peeled and thinly sliced
2 Tbsp. sugar
1 tsp. vanilla

Bookbinding Journal

If you're interested in bookbinding, a journal can be the perfect place to record information on techniques, along with sketches of projects you're working on. A snap to make, my bookbinding journal is a purchased spiral-bound sketchbook with an envelope flap cover.

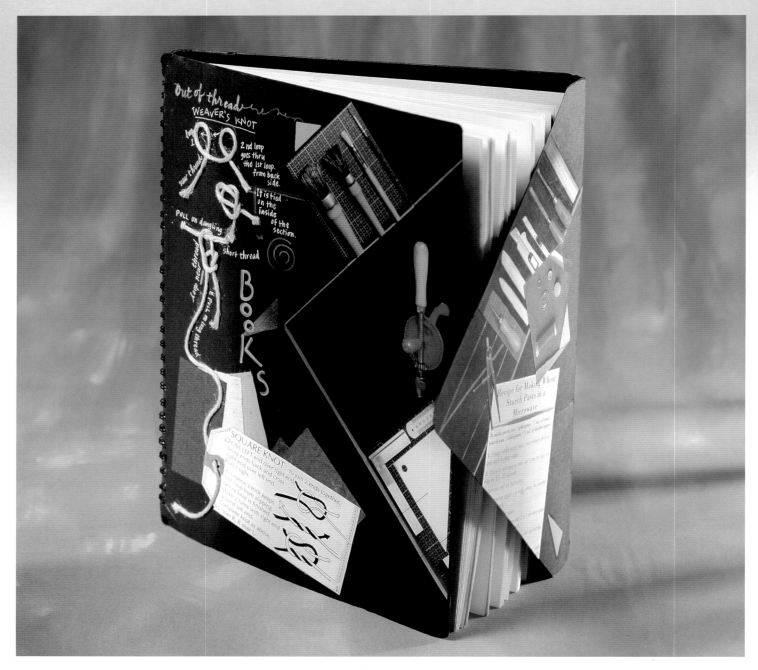

What You Need

Typed instructions for a square knot and a weaver's knot

Linen cord or twine

Scissors

Purchased spiral-bound blank notebook

PVA glue

Gel pens (in different colors)

Book cloth samples

Assorted decorative papers

Manila tag

Color-copied images of binding tools

Recipe for wheat starch paste

Colored pencils

Acrylic paint in colors of your choice

Paintbrush

Decorative elements (colored paper, etc.)

What's Inside

This page includes technical information about making multiple signatures. A second journal page about mending papers is sketched in fountain pen and watercolor.

What You Do

1 Make three stages of the weaver's knot with the linen cord, and without tightening the knots, glue the cord to the front of the notebook. Then use the gel pens to write the instructions for making the knot on the cover nearby.

2 Cut sample sizes of book cloth and decorative papers, and glue them to the front of the notebook in a fan arrangement.

3 Print out the written instructions for the square knot, and glue them to the manila tag.

4 Make the square knot (untightened) with linen cord, leaving one end long as shown in the photograph. Run the long end through the manila tag, and then glue the tag and the cord to the front of the notebook.

5 Arrange the color-copied images of the binding tools and a recipe for making wheat starch paste on the front of the notebook, and glue them in place.

6 Use the colored pencils to draw decorative lines between the images. Then use the paintbrush and the acrylic paint to write the word "Books" on the front of the notebook.

7 Fill in the composition with paint or other decorative elements as desired.

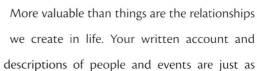

Chapter 3

More valuable than things are the relationships we create in life. Your written account and descriptions of people and events are just as meaningful and evocative as the photos you take of them. Document those funny things your kids say, those special family dinners you sometimes take for granted, and, of course, the antics of your beloved pets. A journal is a wonderful place to explore your family history—it's a privilege to ask another family member to remember his or her life, to reflect back, and to share time together.

Kid Quotes Journal

It really is true—kids do say the darnedest things. And they grow up fast. Once those special childhood years have passed, you can't get them back. This journal is one way to stop time.

What You Need

4 sheets of heavyweight paper (for the accordion), 8¾" x 6¼"

PVA glue and glue brush

2 sheets of scrap paper (waste sheets for gluing)

2 pressing boards, with weights

Metal ruler

Craft knife

Cutting mat

15 sheets of text paper, 8½" x 6"

1 strip of scrap paper (for the 3-hole template), about 1" x 6"

Pencil

Paper clips

Awl or piercing tool

Needle and thread, about 15"

Scissors

2 boards (for the covers), 4¼" x 6"

2 sheets of decorative paper, 5½" x 7¼"

Bone folder

Ribbon

Wax paper

Photo tape

What You Do

To Make the Accordion:

1 The accordion will have eight panels and an overall length of 34" x 6¼" (see diagram A). Fold each sheet of heavyweight paper so its front panel is 4¼" x 6¼" (see diagram B). Every rear panel should have a tab that extends ¼" beyond the fold.

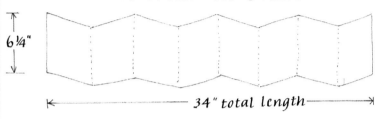

Diagram A

ACCORDION FOLD 8 Panels

6¼"

34" total length

2 To assemble the accordion, you will glue the sections together by the ¼" tabs (see diagram C). Carefully add the glue to the first tab, using the waste sheets of scrap paper to keep the glue line straight (see diagram D).

Diagram B

4¼"

6¼" ←GRAIN→

ea. panel

Diagram C

Glue ¼" tab

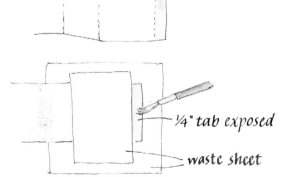

¼" tab exposed

waste sheet

HOW TO GLUE TAB

Diagram D

3 Glue two accordion sections together, folding the tab behind the front panel of the second accordion section (see diagram E). Repeat steps 2 and 3 for the remaining accordion sections; then place the accordion between the pressing boards, under weights, for 30 minutes.

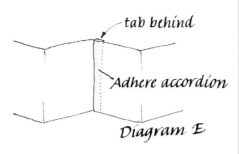

tab behind

Adhere accordion

Diagram E

4 Use the metal ruler and craft knife to trim the height of the book so that all the sections are even (see diagram F). Cut through all thicknesses. See Artist's Touch, page 65, for more on cutting a straight edge.

Diagram F

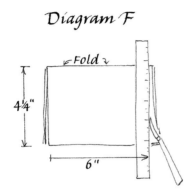

Fold

4¼"

6"

To Attach Text Pages to the Accordion:

5 Fold the 15 sheets of text paper in half (to 4¼" x 6"), keeping the grain in mind. Then separate the sheets into five signatures of three sheets each.

6 Tuck one signature into the first valley fold of the accordion (see diagram G). If the fore edge of the signature needs to be trimmed, see step 4 and diagram F. Then place the accordion and signature between pressing boards, under weights, for 30 minutes.

7 Create the three-hole template by folding the 1" x 6" strip of scrap paper in half lengthwise. Mark one dot in the center of the fold and two more, one on each side along the fold, about 2" away from the center.

8 Place the accordion on a table so that the signature spine is at the edge and secure it with the paper clips and a weight (see diagram H). Place the three-hole template in the center of the signature, and pierce holes in the signature and the accordion.

Diagram H

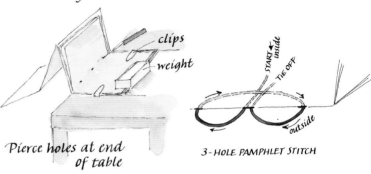

clips

weight

START inside

TIE OFF

outside

Pierce holes at end of table

3-HOLE PAMPHLET STITCH

9 Sew the signature in place using a three-hole pamphlet stitch (see diagram H again). Begin sewing from the inside center of the signature. Loop to enter one of the other holes, follow along the inside spine, go up through the far hole, then loop back into the center hole. Tie the two ends in a square knot on either side of the center thread. Trim any excess thread.

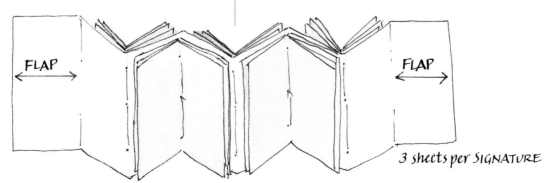

FLAP

FLAP

3 sheets per SIGNATURE

Panels 1 and 8 "Flaps" will attach to covers

Diagram G

To Make the Covers:

10 Cut one set of the boards to 4¼" x 6", paying attention to the grain, to make the front and back covers. Note: You can cut them to be flush with the text block, as I've done, or cut them to include a slight (⅛") overhang.

11 Place one board (the back cover) in the center of a sheet of decorative paper. There should be ⅝" turn-ins on all four sides (see diagram I). Remove the board and add glue to the back side of the decorative paper.

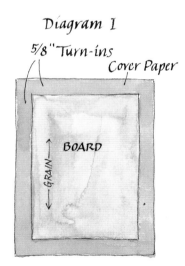

Diagram I

⅝" Turn-ins

Cover Paper

BOARD

GRAIN

12 Position the board on the paper, turn it over, and use the bone folder to gently adhere the face. Then trim the paper corners at 45° angles, 1½ board thicknesses away from the corner (see diagram J).

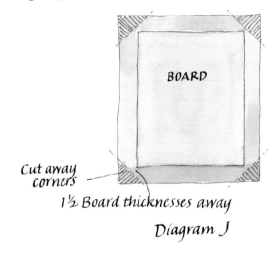

BOARD

Cut away corners

1½ Board thicknesses away

Diagram J

13 Apply glue to the paper and edges of the board; then turn in the head and the tail, followed by the sides (see diagram K). Pinch in the corners (see diagram L). With your fingers, gently pull the paper until it's tight, and then use the bone folder to make sure the edges adhere. Re-glue as needed.

14 Repeat steps 11 through 13 to cover the other board, unless you want to put a window in the front (see below).

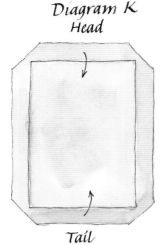

Diagram K
Head

Tail

Diagram L

To Create the Optional Front Window:

15 Decide where you want the window, and then pierce the board from the back with a slit. Mark the four corners, and then cut out the window shape, using a sharp craft knife.

16 Cover the board as described in steps 11 through 13, being careful not to get glue in the window opening. From the back, cut the decorative paper over the window hole in the shape shown in diagram M. Put glue on the back of the loose paper triangles, and pull them through the window to the back. Glue them in place.

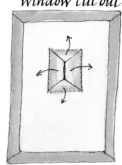

Window cut out

Diagram M

To Finish the Book:

17 Glue embellishments to the front and back covers, as desired, and place them between pressing boards, under weights in a sandwich of wax paper, for 30 minutes. Add a ribbon to embellish the front, and then add two 16" pieces of ribbon to the front and back covers so you can tie the book closed. Position a photo in place so that it shows through the window, and adhere it with photo tape.

18 Center the text block between the covers, and glue the flaps to the inside covers (see diagram G again).

What's Inside

The signatures sewn to the accordion fold include the original artwork made by the children quoted in the journal.

Artist's Touch

Cutting a Straight Edge
Using steady, even pressure, trim through each layer continuously without moving the ruler (see diagram). It isn't necessary to exert a lot of pressure; the cutting blade should be very sharp. The metal ruler should be over the area you're cutting to protect it. The blade should cut away the exposed, uneven edge.

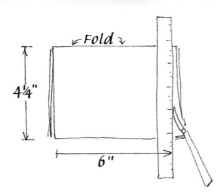

Fold

4¼"

6"

BEATA
At five years old, went up
to Mother and said,
"You are the best mommy
I ever had!"

Family Dinners Journal

One of my favorite journals is filled with drawings and anecdotes from family dinners over the years. Enjoying a plentiful meal with close relatives has become a ritual I no longer take for granted.

What You Need

1 sheet of heavyweight paper, 9⅛" x 15½"

6 sheets of heavyweight paper, each 9⅛" x 11⅞"

Bone folder

Metal ruler

Scissors

PVA glue

Glue brush

2 sheets of scrap paper
(waste sheets for gluing)

2 pressing boards, with weights

1 strip of paper, 1" x 6" (for the spine wrapper)

1 bookbinder's board, 9¼" x width of book
block (for the spine)

Craft knife

Cutting mat

2 bookbinder's boards, each 9¼" x 12¼"

1 large piece of book cloth, 10¼" x 14¾"
(for the outer lining)

Pencil

1 smaller piece of book cloth, 9⅛" x 5"
(for the inner lining)

Wallpaper samples, various sizes

Ribbon (optional)

What You Do

To Make the Accordion:

1 Using the bone folder and the metal ruler, fold one heavy-weight sheet of paper into an accordion shape with six mountain folds (see diagrams A through D). Leave two 1¾" ends on either side unfolded.

HOW TO FOLD AN ACCORDION

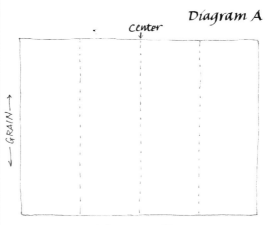

Diagram A

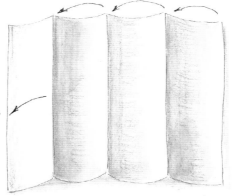

Diagram B

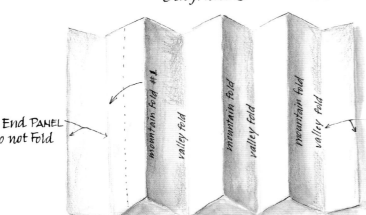

Diagram C

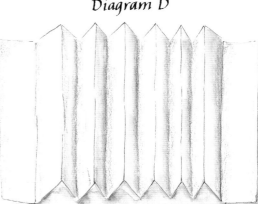

Diagram D

2 Mount each 9⅛" x 11⅞" heavyweight sheet to the left side of each mountain fold (see diagrams E and F). Brush glue onto a fold, protecting the rest of the accordion with the waste sheets (see diagram G). Position the page and set, carefully removing excess glue. Repeat for each page.

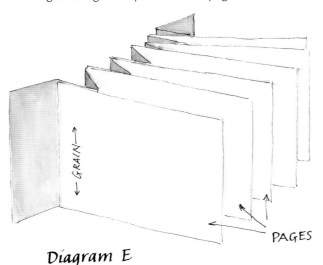

Diagram E

Mount each page to the left side of the mountain fold.

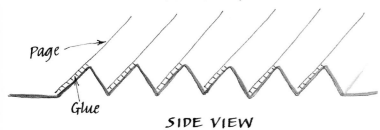

Page

Glue

SIDE VIEW

Diagram F

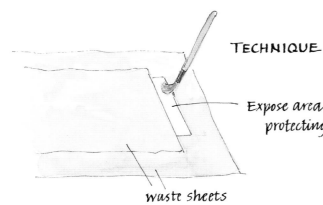

TECHNIQUE

Expose area to be glued, protecting it with waste sheets

waste sheets

Diagram G

3 Place the accordion text block between the pressing boards, under weights. Let it sit overnight.

To Make the Covers:

4 Determine the spine width by wrapping the 1" x 6" strip of paper around the spine of the accordion text block. Mark the thickness by folding the wrapper at the corners; do not pull the wrapper too tightly (see diagrams H and I).

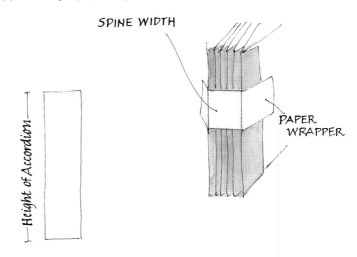

SPINE WIDTH

Height of Accordion

PAPER WRAPPER

Diagram H

5 Cut the spine board to the thickness of the spine wrapper. Its length should be ⅛" longer than the accordion text block or 9¼" long. The two cover boards are the size of the accordion text block with a ⅛" overhang at the head and the tail and an extra ⅜" at the fore edge (total dimensions: 9¼" x 12¼").

To Add the Book Cloth and Assemble the Book:
Note: The book cloth will cover the entire back cover and spine boards, and it will overlap the front cover board.

6 Lay the cover boards and the spine board on the larger piece of book cloth (good side down), leaving ⅝" for turn-ins along the outside edges (see diagram J). Between the cover boards and the spine board, leave a gap the width of two boards. Include 1⅝" beneath the front board.

7 With the boards in place, draw on the wrong side of the book cloth (see diagram J again), outlining the board placement. Remove the boards and apply glue to the book cloth for the back cover board. Place the board back on the book cloth. Turn it over

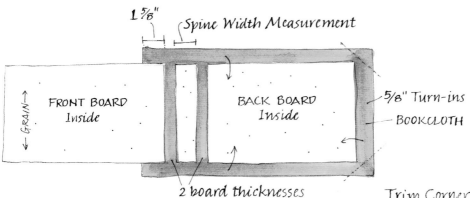

1 5/8"

Spine Width Measurement

GRAIN →

FRONT BOARD
Inside

BACK BOARD
Inside

5/8" Turn-ins

BOOKCLOTH

2 board thicknesses

Diagram J

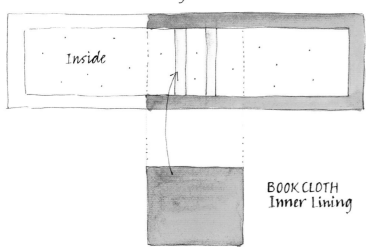

Inside

BOOK CLOTH
Inner Lining

Diagram K

and apply the bone folder. Then glue the spine board and the front board to the book cloth in their proper places using the same technique.

8 Trim the back corners of the book cloth at a 45° angle, about 1½ board thicknesses from the corner (see diagram J again). Turn in the head and tail flaps and glue in place. Turn in and glue the fore edge next, making sure to get glue in the groove of the boards. Apply the bone folder.

9 To make the inner lining, glue the smaller piece of book cloth (good side up) over the inside covers. Center it over the spine so it overlaps about 2" on either side. See diagram K. Apply the bone folder.

Trim Corners

10 Position the accordion text block over the cover's spine edge (see diagram L). Using waste sheets to protect the pages, glue the back accordion flap to the back inside cover.

11 Close the book and place it between the pressing boards, under weights, for 30 minutes.

To Decorate Your Book:

12 Cut a piece from the wallpaper samples to cover the front of the book. Allow a ¾" margin for turn-ins. Glue in place and apply the bone folder.

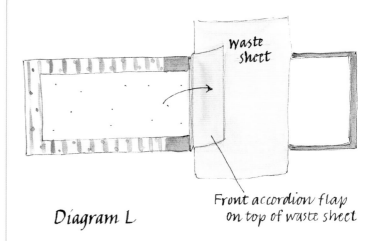

Waste sheet

Front accordion flap
on top of waste sheet

Diagram L

13 Glue the front accordion flap to the front inside cover (see diagram L). Apply the bone folder.

14 Cut pieces of wallpaper to cover the inside front and back covers of the book, leaving a ⅛" margin around the edges. Use as many pieces as you'd like; I used one piece for each inside cover. Glue the paper in place and apply the bone folder.

69

Doggie Journal

Many of us have pets we consider family members—dogs and cats who are dependable, affectionate, and always grateful for the attention we give them. Keeping a journal about a dog is a fun way to remember his or her first ride in a car, all those fun trips to the park, and the silly games you played together.

What You Need

Dog bone template (at right)

Three-ring binder with soft, transparent cover

Scissors

Pencil

Sponge brush

Acrylic paint in yellow ochre, medium brown, and dark brown

Paintbrush

Permanent marker

Card stock (for inside pages)

¼" hole punch

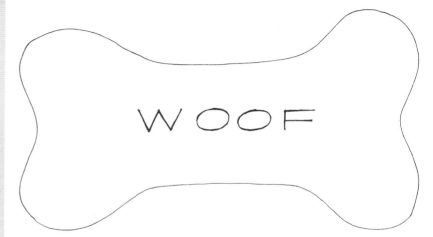

W OOF

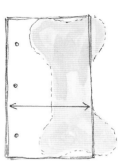

Page width

Diagram B

4 Use the permanent marker or paint to write your dog's name or the word "Woof" in the middle of the bone shape.

5 To make the inside of the journal, cut the card stock pages to the width of the dog bone (see diagram B).

6 Use the hole punch to punch the card stock sheets so the holes line up with the binder rings; then insert the sheets into the binder.

What You Do

1 Enlarge the dog bone template until its length is equal to the length of your binder's fore edge. Cut it out, and use it to trace in pencil the shape along the fore edge of the binder's front and back covers (see diagram A).

2 Cut away the excess material on both covers (see diagram A again).

3 Using the sponge brush, dab the yellow ochre paint along the entire bone shape on the inside of the front cover. Then dab on the medium brown paint, creating a mottled effect as you work. Use the paintbrush with the dark brown paint to outline the edges of the bone, shade the bone, and add a few random flecks. Paint two to three coats of each color.

Cut away excess shape

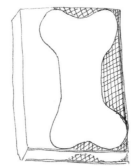

Diagram A

What's Inside

The inside pages of card stock were cut to the outer width of the doggie bone cover. The inside lettering was done with felt markers and colored pencil. A satin ribbon with paw prints lies under the photo.

Pressing Flowers

After your special flower has been chosen, loosen and slide strappings from press. Place papers on press in the following order:

1 sheet of spacer board
1 sheet of botanical paper
flowers to be pressed
1 sheet of botanical paper
1 sheet of spacer board

Cover with press top, slide strappings onto press and cinch snugly. Pressing time for flowers will vary. Occasionally check flowers during pressing and cinch-up straps.

Your flower press contains enough botanical papers and spacer boards to do several pressings at one time. Simply repeat the above steps.

Additional botanical papers are available.

KETCHUM FLOWER COMPANY

Chapter 4

TRAVEL

A travel journal is not only about a place; it's about the journey. The anticipation you feel before starting a trip is the same as the excitement of opening the first page of a new journal. Don't wait until you get home to start your travel diary—make a journal that's easy to take along and record your observations as you go. Describe the scenery, weather, terrain, birds, and anything else that interests you. Jot down thoughts and make sketches. Leave blank spaces to embellish pages later with cutouts from brochures you've collected.

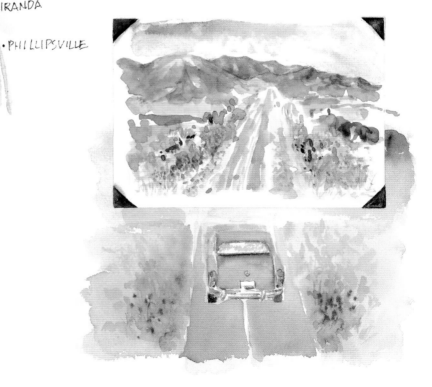

Postcards Journal

Creating a travel journal from the postcards you collect from different destinations is a fun way to remember your adventure. The more postcards you use, the thicker the journal.

What You Need

**Heavyweight paper, postcard-sized
(for hole-punch template)**

Postcards purchased on your travels

¼" hole punch

A strip of paper, 1" x 6" (for the spine wrapper)

**Heavyweight paper, as long as the longest postcard
and about five times as wide (for the cover)**

Pencil

Scissors

Bone folder

Metal ruler

Glue stick

1 set of ledger posts, ⅜" long

Colored pencils

Favorite pens

Scrapbooking embellishments (optional)

Travel watercolor kit (optional)

What You Do

1 Make a hole-punch template out of the heavyweight paper. The hole should be ¼" from the bottom and ¼" from the left (see diagram A). Use the template as a guide for hole-punching each postcard (see diagram B). For portrait-oriented cards, punch the hole in the top left-hand corner. The postcard holes must line up exactly.

2 Stack your postcards, and then wrap the 1" x 6" strip of paper around the stack (see diagram C). The quantity of postcards determines the spine's width. Mark the thickness by creasing the wrapper on the postcard edges, being careful not to squeeze the stack.

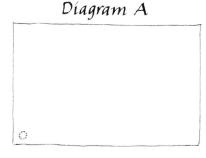

Diagram A

Diagram B

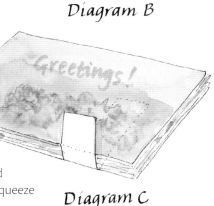

Diagram C

3 Measure the width of your widest postcard and mark it as a dotted line along the length of the heavyweight paper, twice in succession from one edge. Use the spine wrapper to add the spine width determined in step 2, and then mark two more postcard widths. Cut to size if necessary. Your paper should resemble the sample in diagram D.

Diagram D

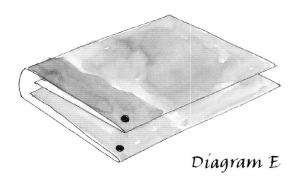

Diagram E

4 Score the heavyweight paper on all fold (dotted) lines with the bone folder and the metal ruler. Fold the cover into shape (see diagram E). Using the punch template, hole-punch the front and back covers. Then glue the inner front and back flaps along the edges. Assemble the postcards within the cover with the ledger posts.

5 Decorate the cover with your choice of scrapbooking embellishments. For example, use watercolor paint to add images or decoupage an assortment of pictures from your trip onto the cover.

Artist's Touch
Being Postcard Prepared

Before you travel, get blank, pre-cut artist's postcards or cut watercolor paper to postcard size. You'll have mini-canvases when you need them to create your own "art photos." Keep a glue stick handy so you can add items like the business cards from shops you want to remember or map sections from a travel guide.

File Folder Journal

Make this handy journal, and you'll be ready to explore any destination, no matter how exotic. Created with a file folder and a series of business-size envelopes, the journal can help you organize souvenirs and keepsakes while you're traveling.

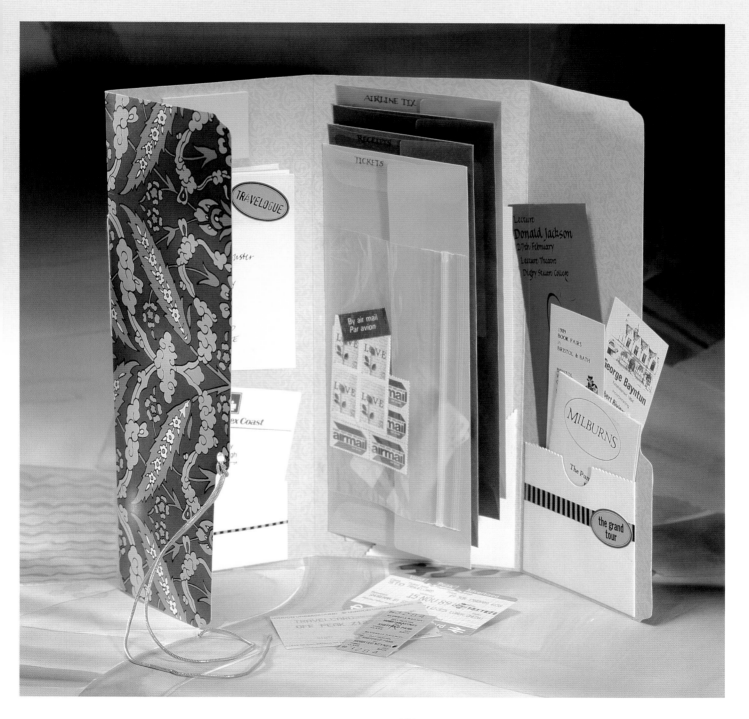

What You Need

File folder

Bone folder

Metal ruler

6 or 7 business-size envelopes

Removable tape

Cellophane tape

Small plastic baggie

Scissors or decorator scissors

Glue stick

4 sheets of text paper, each 4½" x 7"

Awl

Needle and thread

Small sticky notes (optional)

Small calendar

¼" hole punch

Elastic band or cord

What You Do

To Assemble the Folder:

1 Open the folder and measure 4 ¾" from the center fold toward the tab (see diagram A). Score the folder with the bone folder against the metal ruler, and then fold it.

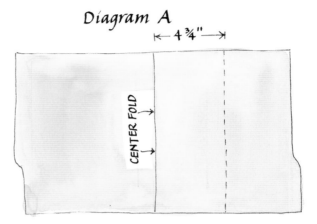

Diagram A

← 4 ¾" →

CENTER FOLD

2 Stagger four or five of the business-size envelopes within the folded section near the center fold, as shown in diagram B.

Stagger envelopes

Diagram B

3 Attach each envelope (flap side up) to the folder on the left edge with a piece of removable tape to temporarily hold in place. Repeat the process, attaching the back of each envelope to the folder. Flip the envelopes to the front side.

4 Use the cellophane tape to adhere the front of the envelopes to the folder. Use enough tape to cover the length of each envelope; then remove the removable tape from the back of the envelopes.

5 Use the cellophane tape to adhere a small baggie for stamps and other small items over the top envelope.

6 Fold the cover over the envelopes at the crease you made in step 1. Now fold it again (see diagram C). Mark and score the flat side of the folder, just past where the fold touches, so you can wrap the folder easily closed.

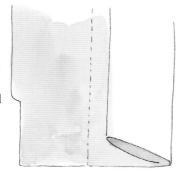

Diagram C

To Make the Pockets:

7 Seal a business-sized envelope, then cut the corner at each end (see diagram D). Glue the envelope ends into position on the bottom edge of the folder (see diagram E) to make pockets A and B.

Diagram D

8 To make pocket C, cut off the bottom third of a business-size envelope (see diagram F), and then glue the envelope into position on the bottom edge of the folder (see diagram E again).

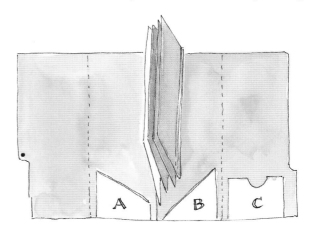

Diagram E

Diagram F

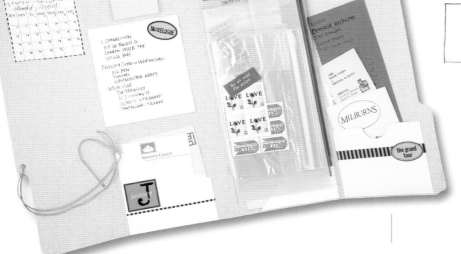

To Make the Signature:

9 Stack the sheets of 4½" x 7" text paper and fold them in half. Align the open signature in the fold inside the left cover (see diagram G).

10 Sew a three-hole pamphlet stitch to attach the signature to the folder. With the awl, pierce three holes—one in the center and one 1½" away on both sides—through the signature and the folder. Begin sewing from the inside center hole. Loop to enter one of the other holes, follow along the inside spine, go up

through the far hole, then loop back into the center hole. Tie the two ends in a square knot on either side of the center thread, and trim any excess thread.

11 If desired, place sticky notes and a mini-calendar inside the cover (see diagram G again).

12 Hole-punch the outer tab of the folder (see diagram G again); then thread an elastic band or cord through the hole to keep the journal closed.

Diagram G

What to Include

Use this File Folder Journal to store both items you'll need as you travel and items you'll want to use in a scrapbook or journal later. Plane and rail tickets, hotel receipts, phone numbers, a calendar, and stamps are just some possibilities.

What's Inside

Vellum envelopes are a great way to color-coordinate your travel file folder. Cut the envelope pockets with decorative-edge scissors. A gold stretch cord holds the folder together.

Unbound Journal
and Travel Portfolio

We may leave on a trip with a thirst for adventure and a blank journal under our arm, eager to describe every sight and sound, but all too often we return home with only a few pages filled. The beauty of the Unbound Journal is that you can create as many or as few pages as you like during your trip and bind them when you get home.

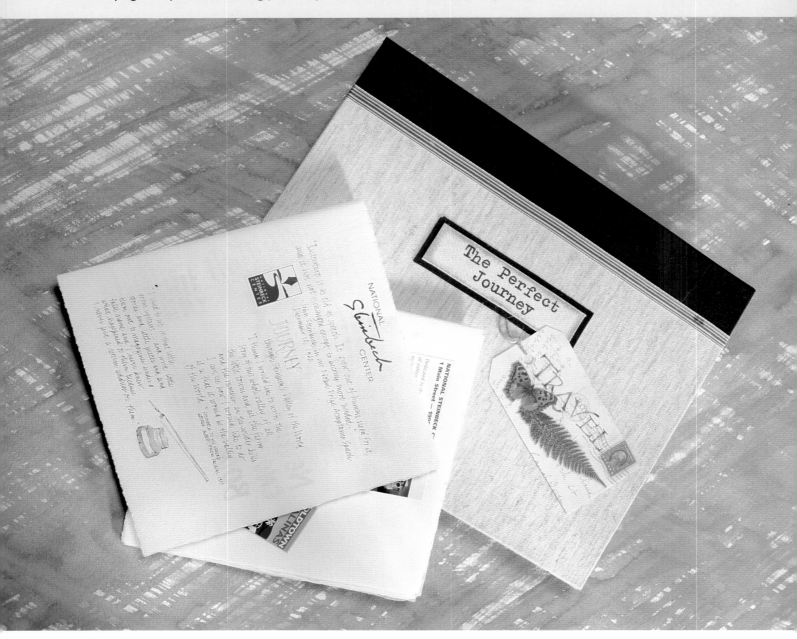

What You Need

Book cloth, 3½" x 12¼"

Pencil

Ruler

PVA glue and brush

2 4-ply boards, each 8½" x 11"

Bone folder

1 2-ply board, 8⅜" x 10⅞"

1 sheet of decorative paper, 9⅝" x 12⅛"

Craft knife

Cutting mat

2 pressing boards, with weights

Wax paper

Elastic cord

Scissors

Tape

Hot glue and hot-glue gun

2 sheets of decorative paper, each 9¼" x 12¼"

Smaller book cloth, 1½" x 10½"

Ribbon

1 sheet of decorative paper, 8¼" x 10¾"

What You Do

1 On the wrong side of the book cloth, measure 1½" from the long side and mark it with the pencil (see diagram A). Measure ½" from the first line and mark a second line.

2 Brush the glue on both sides of the lines, leaving the ½" strip in the center and about ⅝" on the top and bottom free of glue.

3 Place the two 4-ply boards on the book cloth over the glued area, leaving the ½" gap between them (see diagram B). Apply the bone folder to the backs of the boards.

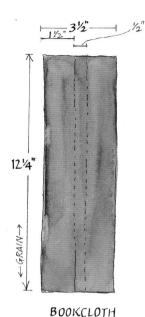

BOOKCLOTH

Diagram A

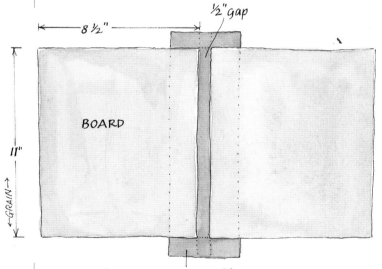

BOOKCLOTH - *wrong side up*

Diagram B

4 Turn in the head and the tail of the book cloth, glue in place, and then apply the bone folder to the ends, making sure the cloth edges properly adhere to the boards.

5 Cover one side of the inner board—the 2-ply board, which is 1/16" smaller all the way around than the 4-ply boards—with the 9⅝" x 12⅛" decorative paper. Trim the corners of the paper at a 45° angle about 1½ board thicknesses away. Turn in the ends and glue in place. Be sure the edges adhere to the board. Apply the bone folder to the glued surfaces and put the board between the two pressing boards, under weights with wax paper, for 30 minutes.

6 Wrap the elastic cord completely around the shorter ends of the inner board (see diagram C). If it doesn't reach or you're afraid it might break, cut the cord to a size that reaches about 1½ times around the board. Pull each cord taut around the front of the board, tape the ends in place on the back, then use the hot-glue gun to permanently affix them to the board (see diagram D).

Diagram C
Elastic Band

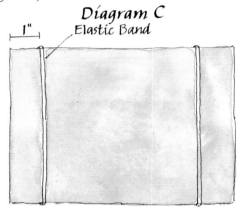

FRONT of LINER

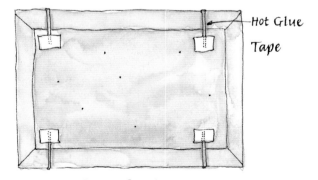

Hot Glue
Tape

BACK of LINER
Diagram D

7 Glue a sheet of decorative paper on the outside of the bottom board. Overlap the book cloth on the spine by 1/16", leaving ⅝" surrounding the other three sides (see diagram E). Turn the board over and apply the bone folder to the surfaces.

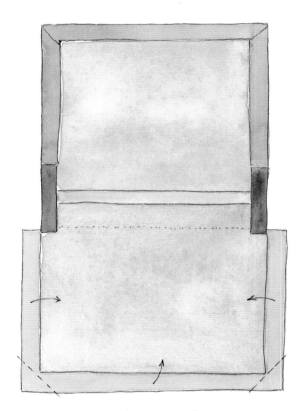

Diagram E

8 Turn the board back over and trim the corners of the paper at a 45° angle about 1½ board thicknesses away (see diagram E again). Turn in and glue the edges, pinching the corners in and making sure the paper edges adhere to the board. Apply the bone folder.

9 Repeat steps 7 and 8 for the top board.

10 Glue the smaller book cloth (1½" x 10½") onto the inside spine, covering the gap between the boards (see diagram F). Bone it well in the grooves.

BOOKCLOTH- *inner lining*

1½" wide

Diagram F

11 Glue the ribbon onto the seam of the front and back cover; then glue the 8½" x 10¾" sheet of decorative paper to the inside of the top cover ⅛" from the board edges.

12 Glue the inner board inside the bottom cover. Cover it with wax paper and then place it between pressing boards, under weights, overnight.

What's Inside

The inside loose signature was done while walking through the National John Steinbeck Center in Salinas, California. The cutout images are from a Steinbeck brochure.

At times we find ourselves in breathless exhilaration and both so very in love

together and promise to support each other's wishes and future dreams.

with each other. We make discoveries together. We hold hands and laugh

For all that has been, Thanks
For all that will be, Yes.
DAG HAMMERSKJÖLD.

Always together and yet each finding the quiet solitude of space separate that brings peace abundant and makes this place sacred for us. I sit on a giant's bench and paint in my sketchbook in the midst of a forest. I watch him put his hands into the silky white waterfall and use his camera artistically to record the most picturesque of framed compositions...

HAPPY ANNIVERSARY GREG. ♡ LOVE, JANET

Chapter 5

LOVE

wrought iron love seat

Matters of the heart are special, whether you're collecting your grandparents' love letters, putting down your dreams for the future, or recording a wedding. Not all love is of the romantic variety: an ongoing journal of the love you feel for a grandchild will be appreciated later by the mother who's busy juggling bottles and sleepless nights. A journal of appreciation commemorating someone, put together with mementos gathered by a group of friends, will be cherished forever.

Hopelessly Sentimental Journal

Inspired by Victorian-era scrapbooks, this journal is a collection of all things sentimental. I made this journal by using jump rings to hinge a cardboard box and lid. Inside, the rings hold pages of keepsakes arranged in plastic coin sleeves.

What You Need

Shallow box with lid

2 clamps

Pencil

3-hole plastic coin sleeves, 8½" x 11"

Awl or hand drill with ¹⁄₁₆" bit

3 jump rings, each ¼" to ¾" in diameter

**Decorative items for cover/lid
(i.e., lace, ribbon, and scrapbook embellishments)**

Scissors

Mat board

Decorative paper

Ribbon

PVA glue

What You Do

To Make the Box:

1 Clamp the lid to the box, making sure the two are side by side (see diagram A). With the coin sleeve as a guide, mark three holes on the inside of the box. Then use the awl or the drill to make three holes through one edge of the lid and one side of the box.

Diagram A

2 Loop the jump rings through the box and the box lid (see diagram B); then add the desired number of coin sleeves.

Diagram B

3 Decorate the inside and outside of the lid and box with your choice of embellishments.

To Make the Letter Holder:

Glue RIBBONS to base

Cover mat board with *decorative paper*

Diagram C

4 Cut a 6½" x 8½" rectangle from the mat board. (Note: You can resize as needed to fit inside your box.) Cover the front of the board with the decorative paper, and glue two lengths of ribbon underneath the board, making sure the ribbons are long enough to tie a bow that will hold several envelopes (see diagram C).

5 Glue the mat board to the inside base of the box.

Love Letters Journal

Everything about a love letter is special—you can hold it in your hands, feel its energy, and read it over and over again. Love can reside in all sorts of letters— in notes from a parent, a sister, a best friend, or a mentor.

What You Need

1 sheet of heavyweight handmade paper, 10" x 23"

1 sheet of oriental paper, 25" x 35"

Pencil

Bone folder

3 sheets of lightweight paper, 9" x 20"

Paper clips

Awl or piercing tool

Needle and thread

Card stock

Scissors

PVA glue

Decorative paper, 9½" x 10"

Decorative paper or fabric (to embellish cover)

What You Do

1 Fold the sheet of heavyweight handmade paper in half lengthwise to create the cover (see diagram A). Set it aside.

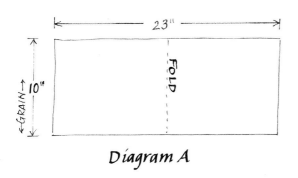

Diagram A

2 Set the oriental paper on a flat surface, with its longest edges at the top and bottom. Make mountain peaks in the paper by folding it 8" from the top, 14" from the top, and 21½" from the top (see diagram B).

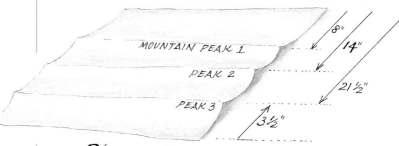

Diagram B

3 Bring mountain peak 1 up to 3½" from the top of the sheet; then crease the paper (see diagram C).

Diagram C

4 Leaving the fold in the paper, bring mountain peak 2 up to 6" from the top of the sheet, and crease the paper again (see diagram D). Then, leaving the folds in place, bring mountain peak 3 up to 6½" from the top and crease the paper (see diagram D again).

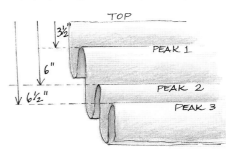

Diagram D

5 Set the folded oriental paper down on a flat surface. Divide it into four sections, as shown in diagram E. Sections 1 through 3 are 11" long; section 4 is 2" long.

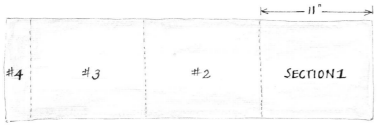

← 11" →

| #4 | #3 | #2 | SECTION 1 |

Diagram E

6 Open the cover and lay the right edge of section 1 of the folded paper against the fore edge of the inside back cover. Lay section 2 across section 1; then create a fold in the paper at the spine and another at the fore edge (back toward the spine). Apply the bone folder to the creases. Fold section 3 on top of section 2. Crease the paper again at the spine. Wrap section 4 behind section 1 and apply the bone folder, creating a short tab (see diagrams F and G).

Diagram F

Inside FRONT

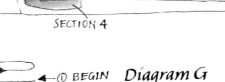

SECTION 3
SECTION 2
SECTION 1

SECTION 4

← ① BEGIN   Diagram G

END →

7 To make the signature, stack the three sheets of lightweight paper, and then fold them in half lengthwise.

8 Using diagram H as a guide, lay the opened oriental paper and the open signature on top of the open cover. Paper-clip the pages together to secure them, and then use the awl to pierce three holes through the signature, the oriental paper, and the cover.

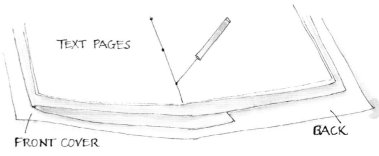

TEXT PAGES

FRONT COVER

BACK

Diagram H

9 Sew the signature and the oriental paper to the cover at the same time using the three-hole pamphlet stitch.

3-HOLE PAMPHLET STITCH

10 Cut the card stock into six strips— each strip should be just slightly smaller than the height and width of a pocket formed by the horizontal folds in the oriental paper. Slip each piece of card stock into its corresponding pocket to provide strength inside the pocket while allowing the beauty of the oriental paper to show.

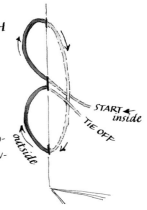

START inside
TIE OFF
outside

11 Stitch the open fore edge of section 1 of the folded oriental paper, catching the card stock inside (see diagram I). Repeat this step for each pocket.

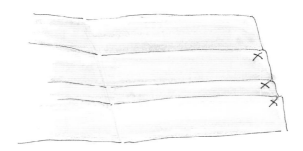

Diagram I

12 Glue section 4 of the oriental folded paper to the back cover; then glue the 9½" x 10" decorative paper over the tab on the inside back cover (see diagram J).

Diagram J

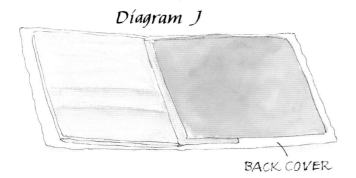

BACK COVER

13 Embellish the front cover with your choice of decorative paper or fabric. Optionally, add a tied letter holder inside the front cover (see diagram K). Now tuck love letters in the pockets inside.

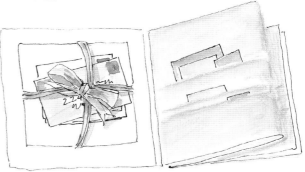

Diagram K

Note: Refer to steps 4 and 5 on page 89 for instructions on how to make the letter holder.

Wedding Journal

It's your wedding day, and you want to capture the feeling of that special occasion—the excitement of the ceremony, the heartfelt wishes expressed in special toasts, the love and encouragement shown by the guests.

What You Need

Sheets of lightweight paper (for text pages), 22" x 8¼"

2 sheets of decorative paper (for covers), 22" x 8¼"

PVA glue

Glue brush

2 clamps

Drill with ¹⁄₁₆" bit

Cord or twine, 16" length

Bamboo twig, painted dowel, decorative chopstick, or piece of wood (for cover)

Favorite wedding photograph

Metal ruler

Bone folder

Ribbon

Wax seal (self-adhering, optional)

Craft knife

Cutting mat

Wedding photographs

Photo tape

What You Do

1 Fold each sheet of the lightweight paper in half individually (see diagram A). You can use as many sheets as you need. Stack the sheets to create a text block. The folded edge is the fore edge (see diagram B); each folded sheet acts as a single page.

Diagram A

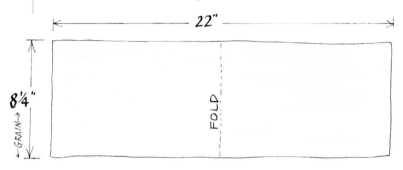

Diagram B

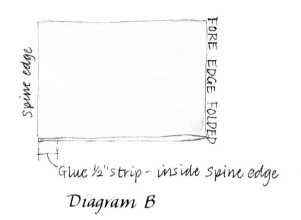

Glue ½" strip – inside spine edge

2 Create all the text pages before you bind them (see What's Inside on page 97); then arrange the pages in order.

3 Fold one of the decorative papers in half to create the front cover. Apply a ½" strip of glue on the inside spine edge (see diagram B again). Repeat to make the back cover.

4 Clamp the covers and the text pages on both sides near the spine (see diagram C). Then drill two holes through all the thicknesses ½" from the spine and 2¾" from the head and the tail.

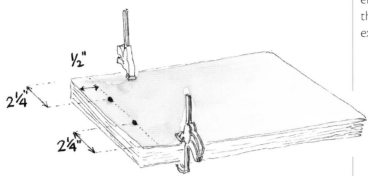

Diagram C

5 Insert the ends of the 16" piece of cord through the holes from the back to the front (see diagram D). Place the twig on the cover over the holes. Loop the cord around the twig twice, re-enter the same holes with the cord, and then tie a square knot at the back with both ends of the cord (see diagram E). Trim the excess cord and add a drop of glue to the knot to secure it.

Diagram D

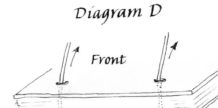

Front

Back

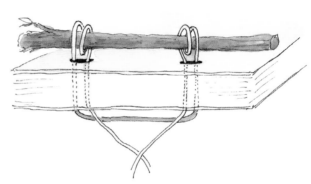

Diagram E

6 Glue your favorite wedding photo to the cover; then "emboss" a frame around it, using the metal ruler and the pointed end of the bone folder.

7 Add two pieces of ribbon and a wax seal with a stamp monogram. I used a self-adhering, pre-stamped seal, but you can make one with sealing wax and a stamp instead.

What's Inside

Each folded text page can accommodate one or more photographs, but leave space for comments, descriptions, and other notes. Using the metal ruler, craft knife, and cutting mat, cut windows in the front of the page to provide a mat effect for your photos to show through. Use photo tape to attach the photos inside the pages. Use as many pages as you need; I used 14 sheets.

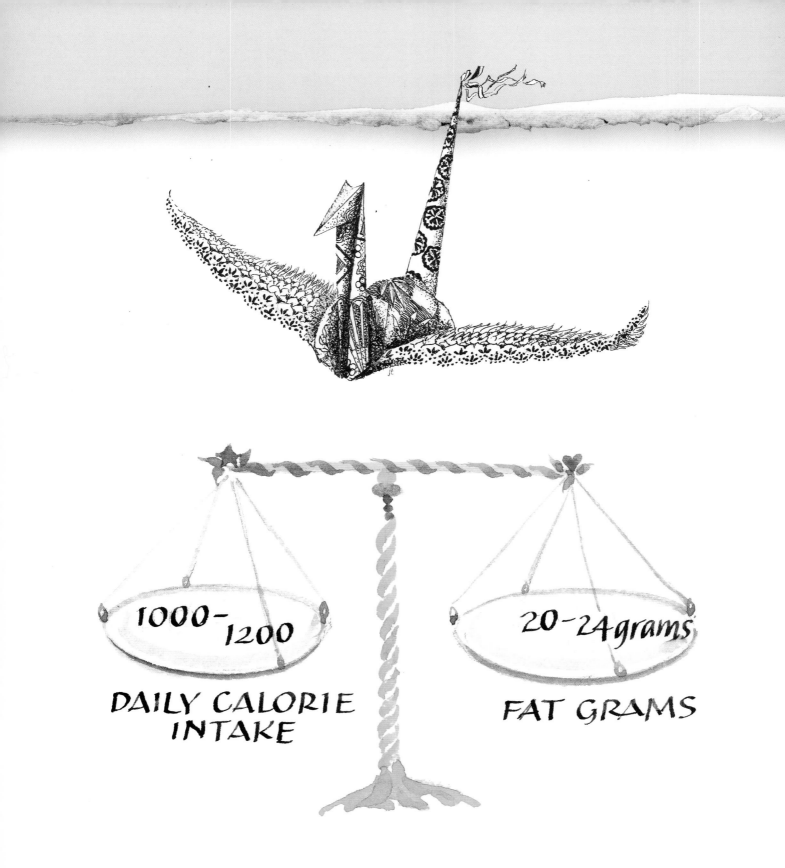

1000-1200

DAILY CALORIE
INTAKE

20-24grams

FAT GRAMS

Chapter 6

HEALTH & WELLNESS

I have found journaling the physical and spiritual aspects of my life to be nourishing. When I was struggling through a challenging time, my Battle-of-Your-Life Journal helped keep me going. A Diet Journal can reaffirm the journey you are making toward a healthier body. The Spirit-Lifting journal is a place where you can jot down stories and quotes that inspire and elevate your spirit. Record things both great and small that contribute to your spirit's well being. Think of this journal as a warm cup of cocoa in the snow or the refreshing spray of a waterfall at the end of a hot summer hike.

WISDOM IS MOST WORTHY

Battle-of-Your-Life Journal

If you're experiencing a difficult time, use the Battle-of-Your-Life Journal to express your feelings and to store helpful information. Decorate the cover with images that will provide encouragement and inspiration.

What You Need

Hardcover journal that appeals to you

Lightweight papers and textured material of your choice

Images that inspire you

PVA glue

Scissors

Twine

Craft knife

Ruler

Pencil

4 sheets of velour scrapbook paper (pink or color of your choice, as large as the journal)

What You Do

1 Tear the images, lightweight papers, and textured material into pleasing shapes, and arrange them on the journal cover in layers. Glue them in place.

2 Cut two pieces of the twine the length of the journal cover. Tie them in a knot, and then glue the twine to the cover so that the knot is near the bottom of the cover. The knotted twine symbolizes your struggles.

3 Cut out the first two pages and the final page of the journal. Then measure, mark, and cut the four sheets of velour scrapbooking paper to match the size of the journal pages. Glue the first sheet of velour paper to the front inside cover of the journal, the second sheet to the first page of the journal, the third sheet to the back inside cover, and the fourth sheet to the last page of the journal.

What's Inside

The inside cover of my Battle-of-Your-Life Journal is lined with pink velour paper and features a photo of Loft, the bear that went with me to every appointment when I was treated for breast cancer. Another journaling page features the ID number from a local cancer 5K walk.

What to Include

- Contacts: As people call with their support, record their names, phone numbers, and addresses. This is especially helpful when writing thank you notes later.

- Exercises and advice that make you feel better.

- Feelings at any given time—fear, hopelessness, gratitude, faith.

- Recommended books.

- Relationships in your life and your support team.

- Suggestions from people who have had a similar experience.

Dieting Journal

Nearly every diet book or exercise plan recommends that you record your progress in a diary. Without a doubt, journaling can be an important part of any weight-loss program. By keeping track of what you eat, you'll feel more inclined to make healthy food choices.

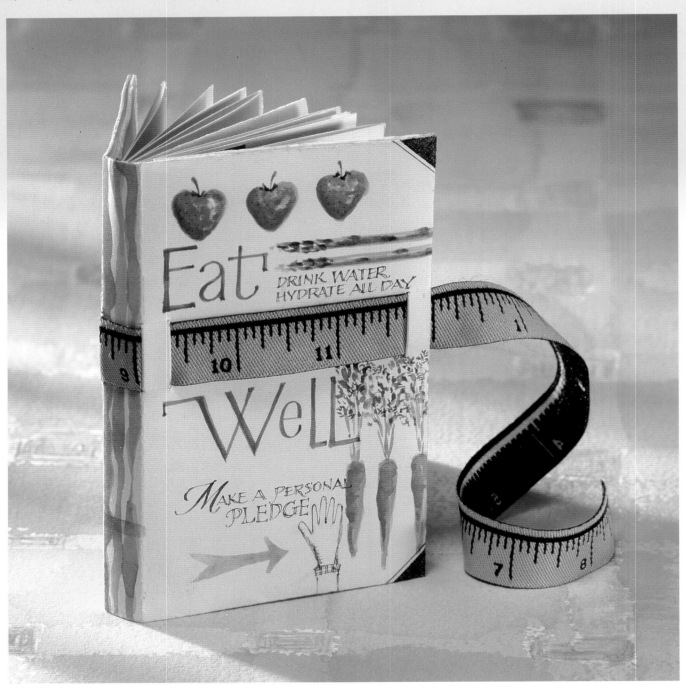

What You Need

1 sheet of lightweight paper, 11" x 17" (for the text pages)

Craft knife

Cutting mat

Bone folder

Images that remind you of your goal

PVA glue

1 sheet of lightweight paper, 11" x 13" (for the cover)

20 inches of ribbon

Pencil

What You Do

To Create the Accordion:

1 Fold the sheet of 11" x 17" lightweight paper in half; then fold it into fourths (see diagram A). Open up the paper, and then fold it into fourths crosswise (see diagram B). The paper will show a pattern of four squares across and four squares down.

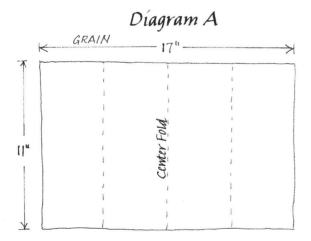

Diagram A

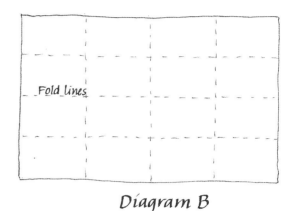

Diagram B

2 Using diagram C as a guide, cut the paper at the designated lines with the craft knife and cutting mat.

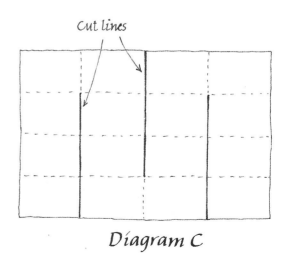

Diagram C

Diagram D

3 Start at one end of the paper and fold the squares back and forth, continuing around to the end (see diagram D). You should end up with a neat little text block measuring 2¾" x 4¼". Apply the bone folder to smooth the folds. Each uncut pair of panels forms a double page. Some will open to the head, some to the tail. On the inner panels that don't open, glue the images you chose—you'll glimpse these as you turn the pages.

To Make the Cover:

4 Fold the sheet of 11" x 13" paper into thirds lengthwise. Lay the text block on its side (without squeezing too hard) to determine the spine width; then make a crease in the cover for the spine fold (see diagram E). Wrap the cover around the text block to make sure it fits—the ends should be twice as long as the text pages—and then open the cover up again.

5 Lay the piece of ribbon (I used one with a yardstick pattern) across the inside center of the cover and mark its width (see diagram E again). Cut slits the same width as the ribbon through all the thicknesses. Then weave the ribbon through the slits (see diagrams F and G).

6 Insert the end panels of the accordion into the open slots of the cover (see diagram H). Apply the bone folder once more. Tie the ribbon to seal the journal.

Diagram E

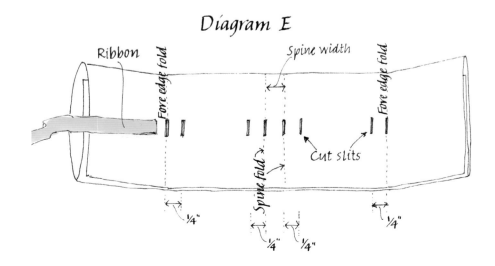

Ribbon

Fore edge fold

Spine width

Fore edge fold

Spine fold

Cut slits

¼"

¼"

¼"

¼"

What to Include

Paste health articles, tips, and quotes that reinforce the diet quest onto your pages. Make special notes near those you have found to be effective. Also include:

A mission statement about your commitment to better health. This statement will help you focus on your goal. Jot down your starting weight on the first page of the journal and your goal weight on the last page.

What you eat—and don't forget quantities. When you write down your daily intake, you can see if a meal is balanced and what might be lacking.

Exercise. Make notes about increased stamina.

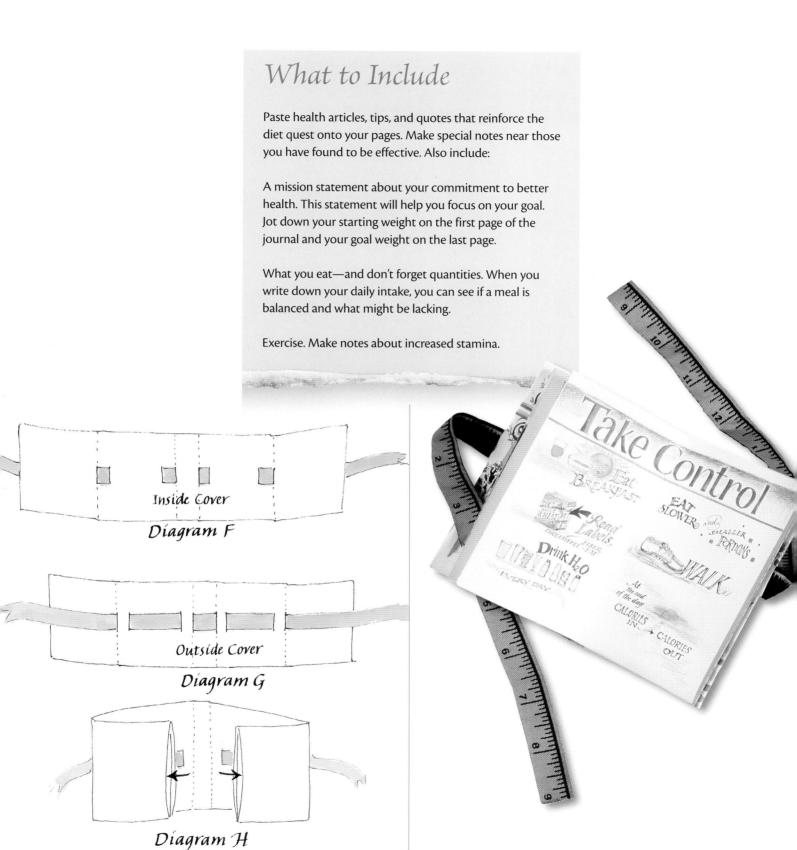

Inside Cover

Diagram F

Outside Cover

Diagram G

Diagram H

Spirit-Lifting Journal

The Spirit-Lifting Journal provides a place to reflect on personal blessings—the things you feel most thankful for. Write essays or poems about the elements that bring harmony into your life.

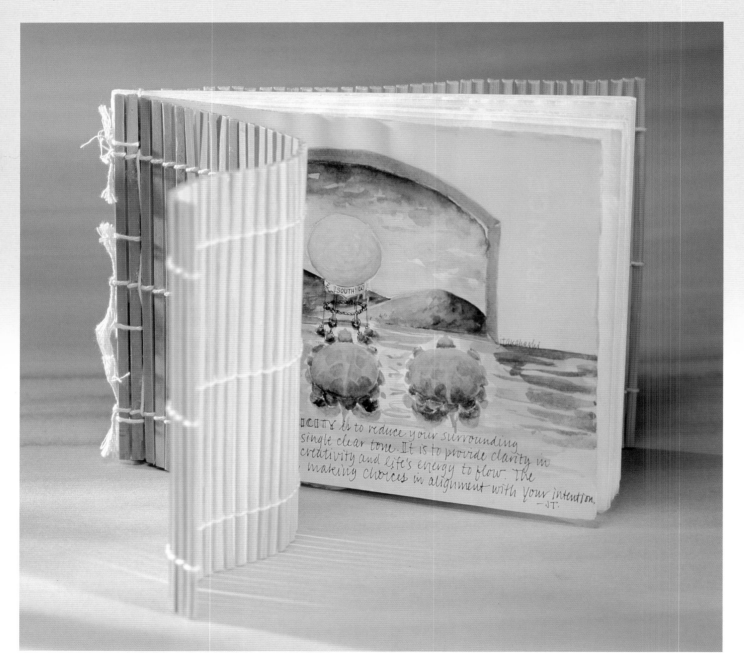

What You Need

Lightweight paper (for text pages)

Scissors

2 small bamboo mats (for covers)

Pencil

Awl or fine drill

2 clamps

Needle and thread (color/texture similar to the bamboo binding)

PVA glue (optional)

What You Do

To Create the Text Pages:

1 Cut the desired number of lightweight papers so they're the same size as the bamboo mats; then stack the pages.

2 Mark four evenly spaced holes ⅜" from the spine. Two holes are ⅝" from the head and tail, and the other two are equidistant (see diagram A). Using the clamps to hold the papers together, drill or punch holes all the way through.

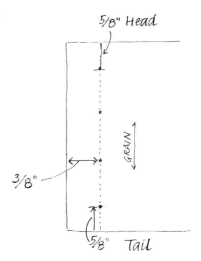

Diagram A

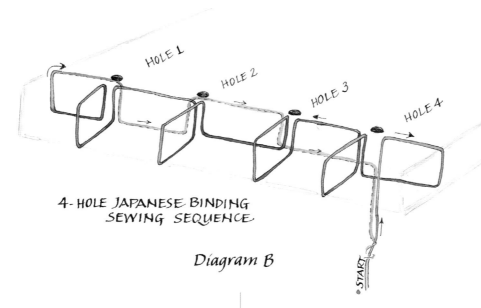

HOLE 1

HOLE 2

HOLE 3

HOLE 4

START

4-HOLE JAPANESE BINDING
SEWING SEQUENCE

Diagram B

To Sew the Pages:

3 Position the stack of pages between the front and back covers so that the left side is flush; then use the clamps to hold the stack together.

4 Sew through hole 4, starting from the back of the book (see diagram B), leaving about 4" of loose thread. Raise the bamboo covers slightly to stitch between the second and third bamboo sticks of each cover.

5 Wrap the thread around the tail and go back through the same hole to the front.

6 Wrap the thread completely around the spine and sew back through hole 4 to the front.

7 Sew into hole 3 from front to back, and then wrap the thread completely around the spine. Enter the same hole to the back.

8 Enter hole 2 from back to front and then wrap the thread completely around the spine. Sew back into the same hole to the front.

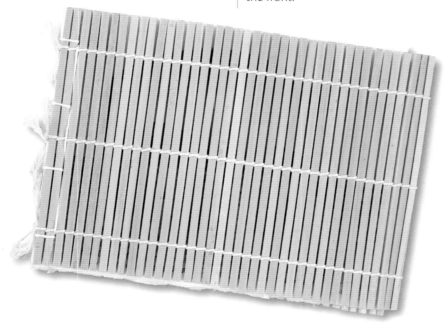

The act of **SIMPLICITY** is to reduce your surrounding environment to a single clear tone. It is to provide clarity in the airspace to allow creativity and life's energy to flow. The clarity comes from making choices in alignment with your intention.

9 Sew into hole 1 to the back. Wrap the thread completely around the spine and enter the same hole from front to back. Wrap the thread around the head and go back into hole 1 from front to back.

10 Sew a running stitch across the back and up into hole 2. Continue across the front and down through hole 3.

11 The sewing end is now at the back. Run the stitch to hole 4 and tie a square knot at the back with the loose thread from step 4. Trim the excess thread. Add a drop of glue to the knot for extra security.

What's Inside

The watercolor depicts three turtles facing the southern morning sky. The next page was scripted with colored pencils and a fine-line pen.

Chapter 7

THE EVERYDAY

Everyday journals both record and generate thoughts, inspirations, and life lessons. These are journals that you make just for you. There's no pressure to decorate each page or turn them into works of art. They are what you grab when you awaken from a dream, feel the need to write down a private thought, or just want to make a quick sketch of something wonderful that life has placed in front of you.

Ideas Journal

Use the Ideas Journal to jot down your creative thoughts and fresh concepts. Later, you can evaluate, edit, or expand on these inspirations. Don't judge them while composing; just let them flow.

What You Need

Heavyweight paper, 8" x 19"

12 sheets of assorted paper (for text pages)

2 large paper clips

Paperweight

Awl

Needle and linen thread

Scissors

Bone folder

2 pressing boards, with weights

Pencil

2 pieces of grosgrain ribbon, each ⅜" x 8"

1 piece of scrap paper (for the sewing hole template), 8" x 2"

2 decorative file folders (for covers)

T-square

Small hole punch (optional)

Craft knife

Metal ruler

Cutting mat

PVC glue

What You Do

Note: This journal has a mix of papers sewn to an accordion fold, with file folders used as covers. The accordion fold is the sewing support, to which you add sewn sections (see diagram A).

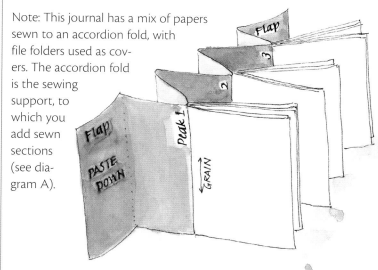

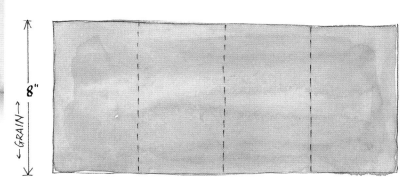

Diagram A

To Make the Accordion:

1 To begin, fold the 8" x 19" heavyweight paper in half widthwise (see diagram B). To complete the folded accordion, refer to step 1 on page 67. The end result should have eight panels with three mountain folds.

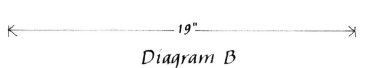

Diagram B

To Create the Signatures:

2 Stack four sheets of the assorted paper; then fold in half. Repeat to create two more signatures.

3 Flatten the first accordion mountain fold and place an open signature on top of it, aligning the inner fold of the signature to the flattened mountain fold. Secure it with the paper clips. Set the piece on the edge of the table with a paperweight on top (see diagram C).

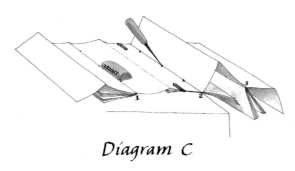

Diagram C

Note: The accordion fold has three mountain folds on one side and four on the other. Sew the signatures to the side with three mountain folds.

4 With the awl, pierce three holes—one in the center and one 1½" to 2" away on both sides—through the signature and mountain folds at the same time (see diagram C again). Repeat this step for the other two signatures and mountain folds.

5 Using the three-hole pamphlet sewing stitch, sew the signature to the accordion fold. Begin sewing from the inside center of the signature. Loop to enter one of the other holes, follow along the inside spine, go up through the far hole, then loop back into the center hole. Tie the two ends in a square knot on either side of the center thread. Trim any excess thread. Repeat this step to sew signatures to the other two mountain folds.

6 Fold the accordion and close the signatures. Apply the bone folder to all the folds, using gentle pressure. Place the accordion between the pressing boards and leave them under weights for a couple of hours.

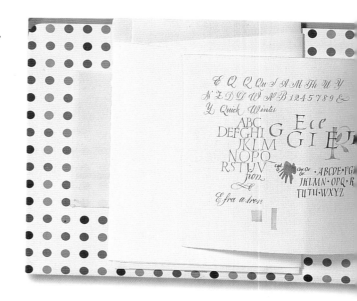

To Make the Sewing Stations on the Accordion:

7 Mark six sewing stations on the spine side of the accordion. The first two marks should be ⅜" from each end of the spine (see diagram D). Then place the two pieces of grosgrain ribbon between the two marks, at an equal distance from each other, and place a mark on either side of each ribbon (see diagram D again).

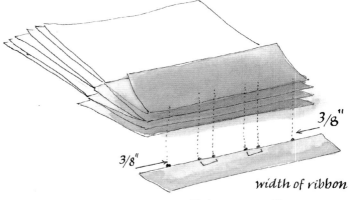

Diagram D

8 To make the sewing hole template, place the piece of 8" x 2" scrap paper against the accordion, and transfer all the marks just made from the accordion to the paper's edge (see diagram D again). Place the template inside the valley fold at the spine of the accordion (between each signature) and transfer the marks there. Pierce the marks with the awl. Repeat this step with the remaining three valley folds, piercing each.

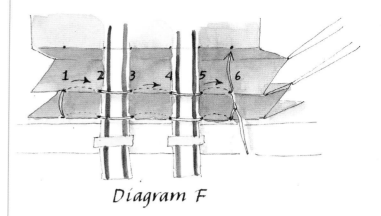

Diagram F

out as before, exiting at hole 6 (see diagram F). Pull the thread taut and tie a square knot with the loose thread from step 9.

12 Enter hole 6 on the third pleat. Continue to lap in and out of the holes, pulling the ribbon through as the thread secures it in place. Then exit hole I at the head (see diagram G).

9 Begin sewing from outside the signature on the lowermost pleat, lifting the accordion as necessary while sewing. Note that the sewing holes are numbered 1 through 6 (see diagram E). Enter hole 6 at the tail end, leaving about 4" of loose thread on the outside. Proceed along the inside fold to the next hole. Exit hole 5 and enter hole 4. Continue by stitching out hole 3 and into hole 2. Exit hole 1 at the head.

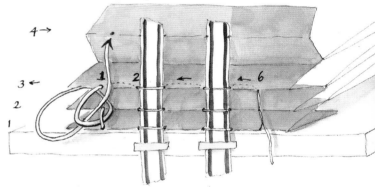

Diagram G

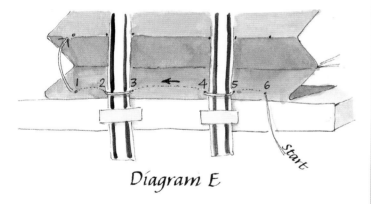

Diagram E

13 Make a kettle stitch by dropping down to the signature sewn just below. Link the needle through the vertical stitch at the head, passing it under the pleat from right to left, towards the head, leaving a small loop of thread. Next, flip the needle through the loop from the bottom up and pull snug (see diagram G again).

10 Insert the ribbons outside the accordion pleat, through the loops created by sewing thread between hole stations 2 and 3 and between 4 and 5 (see diagram E again). Tighten the stitches after each station, pulling the thread in the direction of the sewing, not perpendicular to it, as this will tear the paper.

11 Lower the next pleat, and enter hole 1 with the needle and thread, exiting through hole 2. Stitch across the ribbon, and enter hole 3 with the thread. Continue to sew in and

14 Lower the last pleat (pleat 4), and enter hole I with the needle and thread. Proceed in and out, across the fold as before, exiting at hole 6. Drop down and make a kettle stitch with the signature just below. Because this is the last pleat, do a double kettle stitch. Cut the thread, leaving 1½". Trim the loose thread from step 9, also leaving 1½". Place the accordion between the pressing boards under weights for 30 minutes.

To Make and Attach the Covers:

15 Open one of the file folders, and cut off its upper tab. This folder will be the journal's front cover. Place the spine edge of the accordion against the upper right edge of the folder (see diagram H). Pull half of the two ribbons across the folder, and mark the position of the ribbons on the folder. Then use the T-square to draw lines perpendicular to the spine. Repeat this step with the other file folder to prepare the back cover, except align the spine edge of the accordion against the upper left edge of the open folder.

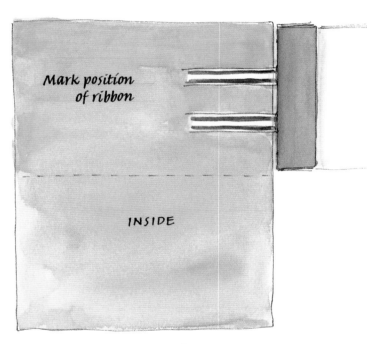

Diagram H

16 Cut six slits in each file folder between the two sets of lines, at ½" intervals (see diagram I). The slits will be as long as the ribbon is wide. To make a clean slit, use a very small hole punch or awl to puncture the ends of each slit; then slice between the holes with a sharp craft knife and metal ruler.

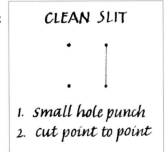

CLEAN SLIT

1. small hole punch
2. cut point to point

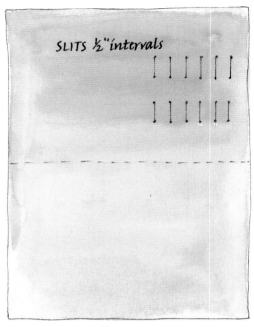

Diagram I

17 For both the front and back covers, weave the two pieces of grosgrain ribbon through the slits—starting from the inside of the book—and pull the ribbons taut.

18 For the front cover only, trim the end of both ribbons, leaving 1" tabs. Keeping the ribbons even and taut, glue each tab inside the folder (see diagram J). Next, glue the loose thread from step 14 and the accordion flap to the folder over the ribbons. With the folder open, trim a sliver off the bottom inside edge (see diagram J again). This will allow the cover to close neatly. Apply a ½" strip of glue along the fore edge, leaving the top and inner edges unglued. You can use this pocket to store notes or more artwork.

19 Close the front and back covers around the book block, making sure the spine is flush. Adjust the unglued ribbons in the back cover. (If you pull the ribbons too tightly, the spine will pinch and the signatures within will splay open. If the ribbons are too loose, the binding may not be secure enough.) When you've found the appropriate tension, carefully open the cover, making sure the ribbons don't move.

116

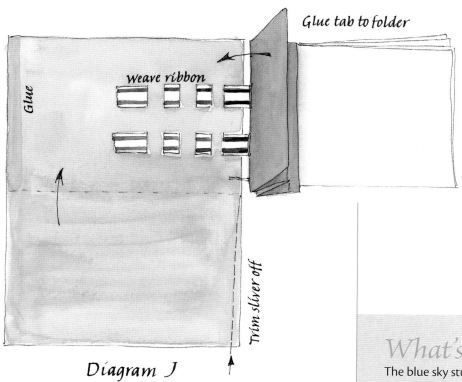

Glue tab to folder

Glue

weave ribbon

Trim sliver off

Diagram J

20 Repeat step 18 for the back cover (see diagram J again).
Then close the covers and apply the bone folder.
You're ready for inspiration!

What's Inside

The blue sky study includes watercolors
and colored pencil studies. This page features sketches for the final artwork of a
magazine illustration.

Dear Diary Journal

Document everyday events as well as record your dreams and wishes.
Use it to write about the week's happenings and how they affected you.
Jot down incidents and memories, insights and reflections.

What You Need

2 pieces of high-density polyethylene-fiber envelope material, 13" x 6½" (for the covers)

Acrylic paints in the colors of your choice

20 sheets of lightweight paper, 13" x 6½" (for the text pages)

1 sheet of scrap paper, 6½" x 2" (for the sewing hole template)

Pencil

2 pressing boards, with weights

Awl

Craft knife

Cutting mat

Needle and thread

3 lengths of strong grosgrain ribbon, 4½" x ⅝"

Removable tape

PVC glue

Bone folder

Wax paper

What You Do

To Create the Text Pages:

1 Stack five sheets of the lightweight paper; then fold them in half to make one signature. Repeat this step to create a total of four signatures (see diagram A).

2 Using the scrap paper, prepare a sewing hole template. Mark the kettle stitch holes ⅝" in from the head and the tail. Mark the next pair of holes ½" in from the kettle holes at both ends. Then mark the next set of holes ⅝" in toward the center. The last pair of holes should be centered on the template, ⅝" apart (see diagram B).

3 Open the first signature and secure it with the weights. With the sewing hole template as a guide, use the awl to pierce holes in the spine of the signature at each mark (see diagram C). Repeat for each signature.

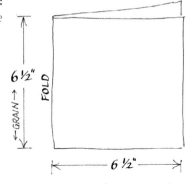

Diagram A

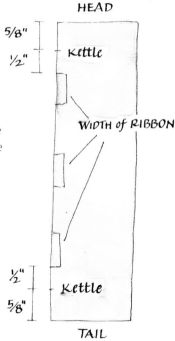

SEWING HOLE TEMPLATE
Diagram B

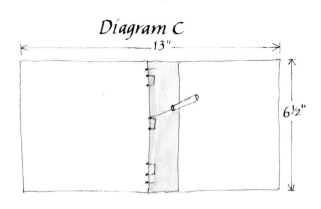

Diagram C

To Make the Cover:

Note: Paint the cover with acrylics. While the paint is still wet, scrape patterns in the cover using combs and other tools. Then let it completely dry before continuing.

4 Fold the two pieces of high-density polyethylene-fiber envelope material in half.

5 Use the sewing hole template and the awl to pierce holes in the fold of the covers (see diagram C again).

6 Cut slits between each pair of ribbon holes on the fold (see diagram D).

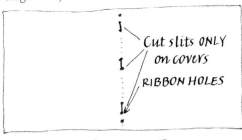

Cut slits ONLY on covers
RIBBON HOLES

Diagram D

To Sew the Cover and the Signatures:

7 Stack the folded signatures on top of one another, spines aligned. Lay the front and back covers in place so that the sewing holes and the fore edge line up (see diagram E). The book should be upside down at this point, with the back cover on top.

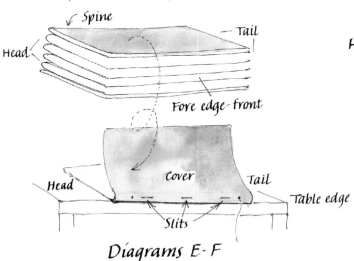

Spine
Tail
Head
Fore edge-front
Head
Cover
Tail
Slits
Table edge

Diagrams E-F

8 Flip over the first signature (the back cover) onto the edge of the table (see diagram F). Open it and weigh it down in place. The book's head should be on the left.

9 To sew the cover, enter from the kettle hole at the tail (right) end, leaving a few inches of loose thread. Proceed inside the entire length of the spine fold, and exit out the kettle hole at the head.

10 Insert the grosgrain ribbon through the slits of the cover and under the sewing thread. Adhere the ribbon inside the cover using the removable tape (see diagram G).

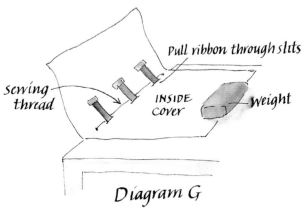

Pull ribbon through slits
sewing thread
INSIDE cover
Weight

Diagram G

11 Close the cover signature and place the second signature (the first signature of text pages) on top. Open it up and weigh it down in place. Sew in and out of the holes, entering the kettle hole at the head, weaving around the ribbons, and exiting at the kettle hole at the tail. Tie a square knot with the loose thread from step 9 (see diagram H).

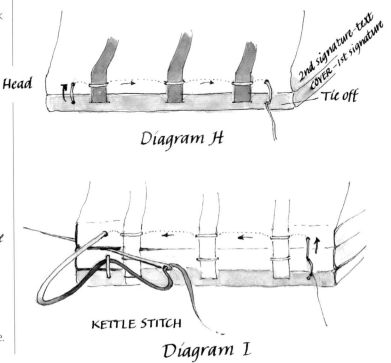

Head
2nd signature-text
COVER-1st signature
Tie off

Diagram H

KETTLE STITCH

Diagram I

12 Close the signature and place the third signature in position, as before. Sew into the kettle hole and continue in and out, being careful not to catch the ribbon while sewing. Pull the ribbons taut and maintain an even tension on the sewing thread. Exit at the kettle hole in the head, and make a kettle stitch to connect it to the first two signatures (see diagram I and the instructions below).

To Make the Kettle Stitch:

13 Slide the needle behind the vertical stitch made when you connected the first two signatures. Then slide the needle between the first and second signatures, and pull the needle out toward the front of the book, leaving a small loop (see diagram I again).

14 Next, bring the needle up through the loop of thread you just created. Pull the needle up tightly and continue sewing (see diagram J).

Diagram J

To Finish the Journal:

15 With the needle, enter the next signature in the adjacent kettle hole. Continue sewing as before around the ribbons, maintaining an even tension on the thread and ribbons as you go. Make a kettle stitch at the end of each row. Repeat this step for each remaining signature.

16 When you reach the front cover, enter the kettle hole and proceed inside the entire length of the spine fold, exiting from the kettle hole at the far end. Insert the ribbon through the slits to the inside, over the sewing thread. Secure it with removable tape (see diagram K).

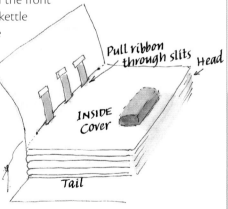

Pull ribbon through slits

Head

INSIDE Cover

Tail

Diagram K

17 Outside the spine, tie a triple kettle stitch, and then re-enter the kettle hole. Tie a knot with the thread already there; then cut the excess thread. For added security, add a drop of glue to the knot.

18 Thread the needle with the excess thread from step 9. Enter the kettle hole of that first signature to the inside. Knot to the thread already there; then cut the excess thread. Add a drop of glue to the knot if you like.

19 One by one, remove the temporary tape holding each ribbon in place. Trim and glue the ribbon to the inside cover, making sure there's enough play in the ribbon for the covers to close easily.

20 Glue all three open edges of the back cover together; then apply the bone folder. Repeat this step with the front cover.

21 Place the wax paper between the covers and the text block. Wax paper acts as a moisture barrier for the glue. Place the entire journal between weighted pressing boards overnight, making sure the spine of the journal is flush with the edge of the boards.

What's Inside

The watercolor pages were done on location during a favorite trip with a field pocket watercolor box. The painting on this page illustrates the quilted bedspread inside the yurt where I stayed.

Sketchbook Journal

They say practice makes perfect, and a sketchbook is the ideal place to experiment with materials, test new compositions, and work on poses and perspectives. Lightweight and functional, a clipboard journal makes it easy to carry your favorite art papers into the field or on a trip.

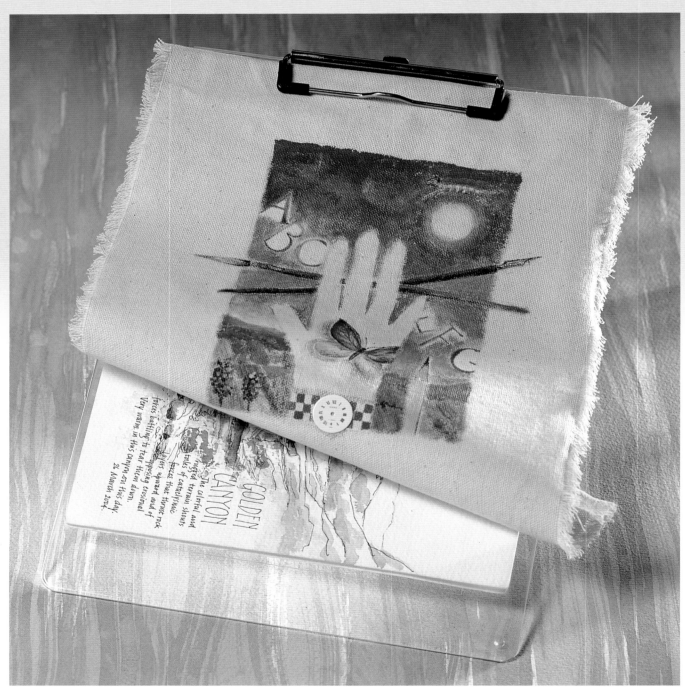

What You Need

Canvas or other material for cover

Letter-size clipboard (with two holes that run from the back to the front behind the clip)

Pencil

Awl

2 eyelets, each ³⁄₁₆"

Eyelet-setting tool

Art supplies and materials to decorate cover

Art paper of choice

Paperclips

Metal ruler

Bone folder

Needle and strong thread

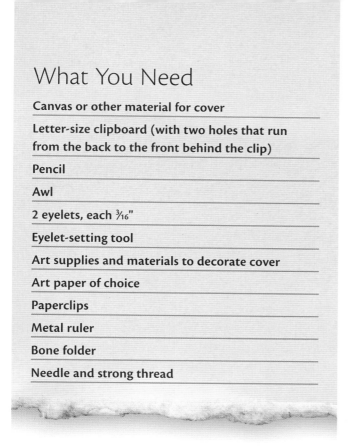

What You Do

1 Fold the piece of canvas to create a 1½" flap at the top. Place the canvas on the clipboard, turn the clipboard over, and use the pencil to poke through the holes in the back and mark the positions for the eyelets on the canvas (see diagram A).

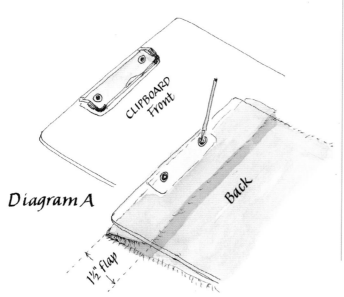

Diagram A

2 Remove the canvas from the clipboard. Use the awl to pierce two holes through the flap of canvas; then set the eyelets with the eyelet-setting tool. Depending on how you plan to embellish your cover, you can decorate it now or wait until the journal is complete. If you decorate it now, make sure it's completely dry before beginning the next step.

3 Stack the art papers wrong side up on the back of the canvas, tucked into the canvas flap. Secure the stack with the paperclips (see diagram B). Pierce the stack with the awl, going through the eyelets and all of the papers.

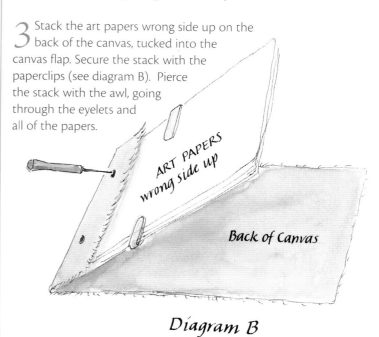

ART PAPERS wrong side up

Back of Canvas

Diagram B

4 Unstack the papers and use the ruler and bone folder to score each sheet of paper 1" from the top (see diagram C). This score line will make the pages turn more easily.

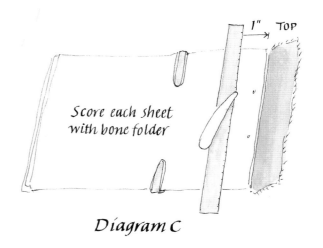

1" TOP

Score each sheet with bone folder

Diagram C

5 Now restack the papers and place them right side up inside the canvas cover. With the needle and thread, start sewing, entering the canvas from the back. Stitch through all the layers of papers, and then exit through the back of the canvas (see diagram D). Don't tie the thread yet.

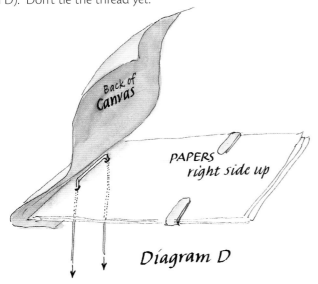

Diagram D

6 Feed the ends of the thread through the holes on the front of the clipboard; then tie a square knot at the back (see diagram E).

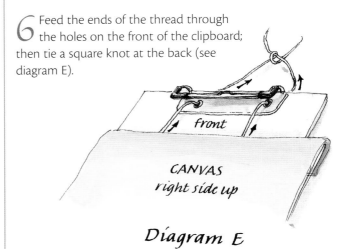

Diagram E

What's Inside

The watercolor pages were done on location in Death Valley, using a pocket watercolor box. The colors in the artist's palette match the color pigments in the Black Mountains.

ARTISTS' PALETTE

Various mineral pigments have colored these volcanic deposits. Iron salt produce the reds, pinks and yellows. Decomposing mica causes the green. Manganese supplies the purple. Colors on the 'palette' are reproduced in a larger scale on the mountains around death valley.

Templates

Nature log template (enlarge 200%)

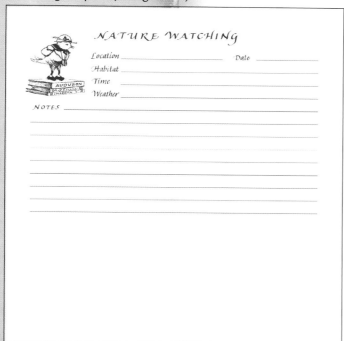

Nature log template (enlarge 200%)

Nature log template (enlarge 200%)

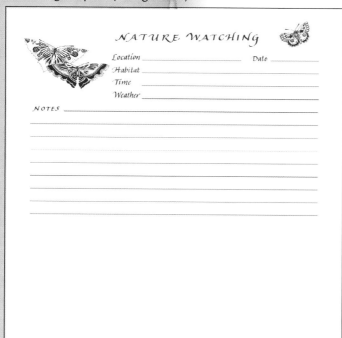

Wheel card template (enlarge 300%)

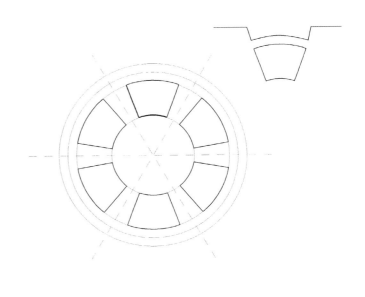

Metric Conversion Table

Inches	Centimeters	Inches	Centimeters	Inches	Centimeters	Inches	Centimeters
⅛	3 mm	3	7.5	13	32.5	26	65
¼	6 mm	3½	8.8	14	35	27	67.5
⅜	9 mm	4	10	15	37.5	28	70
½	1.3	4½	11.3	16	40	29	72.5
⅝	1.6	5	12.5	17	42.5	30	75
¾	1.9	5½	13.8	18	45	31	77.5
⅞	2.2	6	15	19	47.5	32	80
1	2.5	7	17.5	20	50	33	82.5
1¼	3.1	8	20	21	52.5	34	85
1½	3.8	9	22.5	22	55	35	87.5
1¾	4.4	10	25	23	57.5	36	90
2	5	11	27.5	24	60		
2½	6.25	12	30	25	62.5		

About the Author

Janet Takahashi lives life as art. By the age of eight, Janet decided she wanted to be a scientist after she illustrated the solar system with colored chalk. In college, she majored in zoology and botany at California State University Long Beach, taking art classes along the way. Chasing butterflies with a net in one hand and a paintbrush in the other, she realized that art was her passion. She took a class in calligraphy and studied sign graphics at LA Trade Tech in Los Angeles, a class she taught many years later.

Janet has mastered several forms of visual arts including calligraphy, illustration, bookbinding, sign painting, and gilding. She is an avid journal keeper, filling art note pads in a precise, orderly manner using letterforms typically reserved for accomplished calligraphers. Her keen ability to combine calligraphy with illustrations and gilding defines many of her art pieces. Her professional accomplishments include restoring an old Clymer Printing Press (circa early 1800s) and the gilding of a replica of the Palace of Versailles. She has specialized in rare antique sign restoration for celebrities, upscale shopping centers, and major banking institutions.

Janet teaches calligraphy and art at Santa Monica College/Emeritus College and continues to do private commissions and calligraphy for Crane & Co., Tiffany & Co., and Van Cleef & Arpels. Janet resides in Los Angeles, California, with her husband, Greg.

Acknowledgments

*M*any people have contributed to the nourishment and journey of this book. I am so very grateful and would especially like to acknowledge the following people. I bow to you in humble gratitude.

to my mother, Mary Takahashi, for her constant love. She taught me how to live with grace and strength and to always explore my imagination.

to my father, Frank Takahashi, for teaching me to be independent, think creatively, and always live life beyond the box.

to Cathy Risling, my editor, who initially held me by the hand, supporting and pushing to keep me on schedule. She became my friend and saw my projects to the end.

to Kathy Sheldon, editor extraordinaire at Lark Books, whose creative vision and support has made all the difference in the world. She inspired me through a most difficult time. Artful mastery at work.

to all the staff at Lark Books—Chris Bryant, Julie Hale, Mark Bloom, Susan McBride, and Shannon Yokeley—for their expertise, attention to detail, and artful saavy while still maintaining enthusiasm on my project. What a team!

to family members Kachi Takahashi, Naomi and John Sweredoski, Gilda and Irv Kushner, Robin and Howard Goldberg, and Sarah and Michael: their precious energy, love, and positive support is without a doubt always present.

to friends Linda Anderson, Nancy McCarthy, Helen Gershen, Marie Lewis, and Barbara Wood: for listening patiently to my writings at any hour, and for providing their honest comments, critiques, and words of encouragement that only good friends can give.

and to friends Louise Hasegawa, Cookie Atsumi, and Eva Kuwata, for all the comfort dinners and uncountable kindnesses that they brought into my life.

to my students in the Calligraphy class at Emeritus College, who continue to inspire and teach me more about creativity and living an artful life. And to Maggie Hall, Associate Dean of Emeritus College of Santa Monica College, who has given me the opportunity to teach—it has been a gift.

to my support team: Dr. John Butler, UC Irvine Hospital, surgeon; Dr. Cynthia Forsthoff, oncologist; Sandra Hernandez, Geri Hing, Lyle Young, Tosh, and Amy Shinden; Geri Bieber, Ruth Merritt, Nancy Stoll, Abella Carroll, Gene McCarthy, Cathy and Dave Kaihara, and Russell Nakada. They aided my recovery, were on my wellness team, and continue to be an inspiration to me. Every day is sacred and is only better when shared.

special thanks to Noah & Nancy Mackenroth; Beata, Henia, and Renatta; artist Linda Gunn; Diane Ide and Summer; Janey Saavedra; Joe McGrade; Hiromi Katayama of Hiromi Paper International for all the beautiful Japanese rice papers; Scrampers Scrapbooking; papermaker Margaret Sahlstrand, Icosa Studio; artist Helen Rasplicka of San Antonio for her handmade paper cover used for the Love Letters journal; naturalist Jack Ellwanger of Pelican Network and Big Sur Lodge; my friends at Treebones Resort in Big Sur; and my friend Virginia Gardner in Santa Barbara for setting me on the botanical path that sustains me. Their expertise and passions are truly celebrations.

and to my husband, Gregory Minuskin, for his rock-solid support, honesty, love, and endless patience. For sharing the poetry of nature, and for making every minute of time a journey that is an artist's dream.

to my Mother and the memory of my Father, and to my husband, Gregory

Index